CRYPTOGRAPHY AND COMPUTER SCIENCE

DESIGN MANUAL FOR ALGORITHMS, CODES AND CIPHERS

4 BOOKS IN 1

BOOK 1
INTRODUCTION TO CRYPTOGRAPHY: A BEGINNER'S GUIDE

BOOK 2
CRYPTOGRAPHIC ALGORITHMS AND PROTOCOLS: A COMPREHENSIVE GUIDE

BOOK 3
ADVANCED CRYPTANALYSIS: BREAKING CODES AND CIPHERS

BOOK 4
CUTTING-EDGE CRYPTOGRAPHY: EMERGING TRENDS AND FUTURE DIRECTIONS

ROB BOTWRIGHT

Published by Rob Botwright
Library of Congress Cataloging-in-Publication Data
ISBN 978-1-83938-552-0
Cover design by Rizzo

Disclaimer

The contents of this book are based on extensive research and the best available historical sources. However, the author and publisher make no claims, promises, or guarantees about the accuracy, completeness, or adequacy of the information contained herein. The information in this book is provided on an "as is" basis, and the author and publisher disclaim any and all liability for any errors, omissions, or inaccuracies in the information or for any actions taken in reliance on such information.

The opinions and views expressed in this book are those of the author and do not necessarily reflect the official policy or position of any organization or individual mentioned in this book. Any reference to specific people, places, or events is intended only to provide historical context and is not intended to defame or malign any group, individual, or entity.

The information in this book is intended for educational and entertainment purposes only. It is not intended to be a substitute for professional advice or judgment. Readers are encouraged to conduct their own research and to seek professional advice where appropriate.

Every effort has been made to obtain necessary permissions and acknowledgments for all images and other copyrighted material used in this book. Any errors or omissions in this regard are unintentional, and the author and publisher will correct them in future editions.

TABLE OF CONTENTS – BOOK 1 - INTRODUCTION TO CRYPTOGRAPHY: A BEGINNER'S GUIDE

TABLE OF CONTENTS – BOOK 2 - CRYPTOGRAPHIC ALGORITHMS AND PROTOCOLS: A COMPREHENSIVE GUIDE

TABLE OF CONTENTS – BOOK 3 - ADVANCED CRYPTANALYSIS: BREAKING CODES AND CIPHERS

TABLE OF CONTENTS – BOOK 4 - CUTTING-EDGE CRYPTOGRAPHY: EMERGING TRENDS AND FUTURE DIRECTIONS

Introduction

Welcome to the fascinating world of "Cryptography and Computer Science: Design Manual for Algorithms, Codes, and Ciphers," an extraordinary journey through the realms of digital secrecy, protection, and innovation. This comprehensive book bundle encompasses a spectrum of knowledge, from the foundational principles of cryptography to the cutting-edge technologies shaping its future. With four distinct volumes at your fingertips, this bundle invites you to explore the depths of encryption, decryption, cryptanalysis, and the exciting emerging trends in the ever-evolving world of computer science and cryptography.

Book 1 - Introduction to Cryptography: A Beginner's Guide
Our journey begins with the foundational volume, "Introduction to Cryptography: A Beginner's Guide." This book is your stepping stone into the intricate universe of cryptography, tailored to make even the most complex concepts accessible to newcomers. Whether you're a novice or an enthusiast, this guide demystifies encryption, decryption, keys, and the fundamental principles that underpin the security of our digital world.

Book 2 - Cryptographic Algorithms and Protocols: A Comprehensive Guide
In "Cryptographic Algorithms and Protocols: A Comprehensive Guide," we take a deeper dive into the core of cryptography. This volume explores a rich tapestry of cryptographic algorithms and protocols that have shaped the digital security landscape. From the timeless symmetric key cryptography to the revolutionary world of asymmetric cryptography, from block ciphers to stream ciphers, this book leaves no stone unturned. Discover the inner workings of the protocols that secure our online communications, transactions, and data storage, equipping you with a comprehensive understanding of cryptographic tools at your disposal.

Book 3 - Advanced Cryptanalysis: Breaking Codes and Ciphers
With newfound knowledge, we shift our focus to cryptanalysis in "Advanced Cryptanalysis: Breaking Codes and Ciphers." Here, we explore the art of deciphering encrypted messages, probing the weaknesses of cryptographic systems, and understanding the perpetual battle between cryptographers and cryptanalysts. Classical and contemporary cryptanalysis techniques come to life as we uncover the secrets of code-breaking. This volume empowers you to think like a cryptanalyst, sharpening your skills in the intriguing world of codebreaking.

Book 4 - Cutting-Edge Cryptography: Emerging Trends and Future Directions
Our journey culminates in "Cutting-Edge Cryptography: Emerging Trends and Future Directions," where we project ourselves into the future of cryptography. Here, we examine the imminent threat of quantum computing and the race to develop post-quantum cryptography. We delve into the exciting realms of homomorphic encryption, multi-party computation, and zero-knowledge proofs, envisioning a world where cryptography continues to evolve and adapt to the dynamic digital landscape.

Together, these four volumes serve as your indispensable guide to the intricate world of cryptography and its symbiotic relationship with computer science. Whether you're a curious beginner or an experienced professional, this book bundle promises to unlock the secrets of digital security, challenge your intellect, and prepare you for the thrilling journey ahead.

So, embark on this enlightening expedition through "Cryptography and Computer Science: Design Manual for Algorithms, Codes, and Ciphers," and prepare to unravel the mysteries of the digital realm like never before.

BOOK 1
INTRODUCTION TO CRYPTOGRAPHY
A BEGINNER'S GUIDE

ROB BOTWRIGHT

Chapter 1: The World of Cryptography

Cryptography, the science of securing information through mathematical techniques, plays an indispensable role in modern society. It's a field that combines mathematics, computer science, and engineering to protect data and communications from unauthorized access and manipulation. Cryptographic techniques are used in everyday activities, often without people even realizing it. From online banking and shopping to sending private messages, cryptography is an essential guardian of digital privacy and security.

Cryptography has a rich history, dating back to ancient civilizations where it was used to encode sensitive information and protect it from adversaries. Over the centuries, cryptographic methods evolved from simple substitution ciphers to complex algorithms that form the foundation of modern encryption.

In today's interconnected world, data is constantly in transit over networks, making it vulnerable to interception by malicious actors. This is where cryptography steps in. Cryptographic algorithms transform plaintext data into ciphertext, rendering it unreadable to anyone without the proper decryption key. The confidentiality provided by encryption is crucial in safeguarding sensitive information such as financial transactions, medical records, and personal communications.

One of the fundamental concepts in cryptography is the use of keys. Keys are essentially secret values that determine how data is encrypted and decrypted. In symmetric key cryptography, the same key is used for both encryption and decryption, while in asymmetric key cryptography, a pair of keys—one public and one private—is used to facilitate secure communication. The mathematical relationship between these keys ensures that information encrypted with one key can only be decrypted with its corresponding key.

As technology advances, so do the cryptographic techniques used to protect data. Cryptanalysis, the study of breaking cryptographic systems, is an ever-present challenge. With the advent of powerful computers and the potential threat posed by quantum computing, researchers are continually developing new cryptographic algorithms and strategies to stay ahead of potential threats.

The historical foundations of cryptography are fascinating. Ancient civilizations like the Egyptians and Greeks employed simple substitution ciphers to conceal the meaning of their messages. The famous Caesar cipher, named after Julius Caesar, involved shifting letters in the alphabet to create a ciphertext. While these methods were relatively straightforward, they served their purpose in preserving the secrecy of critical information.

Over time, cryptographic techniques became more sophisticated. During World War II, the Enigma machine used by the Axis powers was a significant cryptographic challenge for the Allies. The successful decryption of Enigma-encrypted messages by British codebreakers, including Alan Turing, played a pivotal role in the war's outcome.

As the digital age dawned, the need for secure communication across computer networks became apparent. This led to the development of modern cryptography, which encompasses a wide range of techniques and applications. Symmetric ciphers like the Data Encryption Standard (DES) and Advanced Encryption Standard (AES) became essential for encrypting data at rest and in transit.

Public Key Infrastructure (PKI) introduced the concept of asymmetric encryption, allowing secure communication over untrusted networks. PKI relies on digital certificates issued by trusted authorities to verify the identity of parties involved in a transaction. This technology underpins secure web browsing and email encryption, ensuring that data exchanged online remains confidential and secure.

The evolution of cryptography has not been without challenges. Cryptanalysts constantly seek weaknesses in cryptographic systems, leading to a perpetual cycle of innovation and defense. Researchers are also addressing the threat posed by quantum computing, which has the potential to break many of the encryption methods used today. This has spurred the development of post-quantum cryptography, which aims to provide secure alternatives resistant to quantum attacks.

Cryptographic algorithms are not limited to data protection alone; they also play a crucial role in digital signatures. Digital signatures are electronic equivalents of handwritten signatures, providing authentication and non-repudiation in digital transactions. They are widely used in applications like electronic contracts, legal documents, and software distribution.

Secure communication protocols are the backbone of secure online interactions. Protocols like SSL/TLS ensure the confidentiality and integrity of data transmitted between web browsers and servers. This encryption helps prevent eavesdropping and data tampering during online transactions, creating a secure environment for activities like online shopping and banking.

Cryptographic hash functions are essential tools in ensuring data integrity. These one-way mathematical functions take input data and produce a fixed-size hash value. Even a minor change in the input data results in a vastly different hash value. Hash functions are used to verify the integrity of files and messages, providing a way to detect any unauthorized alterations.

The advent of blockchain technology has brought cryptography into the realm of digital currencies like Bitcoin. Blockchain relies heavily on cryptographic techniques to secure transactions and ensure the immutability of the ledger. Through a decentralized network of nodes and cryptographic hashing, blockchain enables trustless peer-to-peer transactions.

Zero-knowledge proofs are a fascinating cryptographic concept that allows one party to prove to another that they know a specific piece of information without revealing the information itself. This technology has far-reaching applications, from secure authentication without revealing passwords to ensuring privacy in various types of transactions.

Biometric cryptosystems merge biometric data like fingerprints or retinal scans with cryptographic keys to enhance security. Biometrics provide an additional layer of authentication, making it extremely difficult for unauthorized users to gain access to sensitive systems or data.

The Internet of Things (IoT) and edge computing are transforming the way we interact with the digital world.

Cryptographic protocols tailored to these environments ensure that devices can communicate securely and that data remains protected even in decentralized and resource-constrained settings.

Beyond the technical aspects, cryptography also raises important ethical and societal questions. The balance between privacy and security is a perennial debate, as governments and organizations grapple with the need to protect citizens and users while respecting individual rights to privacy.

In summary, cryptography has evolved from ancient techniques to become a cornerstone of modern society. Its applications are vast and touch nearly every aspect of our digital lives. The ongoing quest to stay ahead of cryptographic threats and the ethical considerations surrounding its use make cryptography a dynamic and essential field in the digital age.

As we delve deeper into the world of cryptography, it's essential to familiarize ourselves with the terminology and fundamental concepts that underpin this fascinating field. Cryptography, in its simplest form, is the art and science of securing information through mathematical techniques. It's a multifaceted discipline that encompasses a wide range of methods and principles, all aimed at protecting data from unauthorized access and ensuring its confidentiality, integrity, and authenticity.

One of the fundamental concepts in cryptography is encryption, a process that transforms plaintext data into ciphertext. This ciphertext appears as a jumble of characters and is designed to be unreadable to anyone without the appropriate decryption key. The primary objective of encryption is to ensure that sensitive information remains confidential during transmission or storage.

To achieve encryption, cryptographic algorithms are employed. These algorithms are sets of mathematical rules and operations that determine how data is transformed from plaintext to ciphertext and vice versa. Symmetric key cryptography and asymmetric key cryptography are two primary categories of cryptographic algorithms, each with its unique characteristics and use cases.

In symmetric key cryptography, the same key is used for both encryption and decryption. This key, often referred to as a shared secret key, must remain confidential between the sender and receiver. The simplicity of symmetric encryption makes it efficient for encrypting large volumes of data, such as files and messages. However, key management and distribution can pose significant challenges.

Asymmetric key cryptography, on the other hand, relies on a pair of keys—an encryption key and a decryption key. The encryption key is public and can be freely shared, while the decryption key remains private. This approach facilitates secure communication between parties who have never met or exchanged keys before. Digital signatures, a critical component of many cryptographic systems, are also based on asymmetric key cryptography.

Public and private keys form the core of asymmetric key cryptography. When someone wants to send you an encrypted message, they use your public key to encrypt it. Only you, possessing the corresponding private key, can decrypt and read the message. This asymmetry in key usage provides a robust method for secure communication over open networks.

A related concept in cryptography is key management. Managing cryptographic keys is essential to maintaining the security of encrypted data. It involves key generation, distribution, storage, and rotation. Secure key management ensures that keys are protected from unauthorized access and loss.

In the realm of cryptography, we often encounter the term "cryptanalysis." Cryptanalysis is the study of breaking cryptographic systems. It involves analyzing cryptographic algorithms and attempting to find vulnerabilities or weaknesses that can be exploited to recover the plaintext from ciphertext without knowledge of the key. Cryptanalysts employ various techniques, including mathematical analysis and computational methods, to decrypt encrypted data.

Now, let's discuss the concept of a cryptographic protocol. A cryptographic protocol is a set of rules and procedures that dictate how cryptographic algorithms are used to achieve specific security objectives. These protocols are often used in secure communication over networks. For instance, the Secure Sockets Layer (SSL) and its successor, Transport Layer Security (TLS), are cryptographic protocols that provide secure data transmission over the internet, ensuring the confidentiality and integrity of data exchanged between web browsers and servers.

When we talk about encryption, it's crucial to differentiate between two encryption modes: symmetric encryption and asymmetric encryption. In symmetric encryption, the same key is used for both encryption and decryption, making it relatively straightforward but requiring secure key exchange between communicating parties. Asymmetric encryption uses a pair of keys, one for encryption and the other for decryption, offering greater security and convenience in key exchange but at a computational cost.

Hash functions are another integral part of the cryptographic toolbox. A cryptographic hash function takes an input, often of variable length, and produces a fixed-size string of characters, which is typically a hexadecimal number. These hash values are unique to the input data and appear random, even if the input only changes slightly. Hash functions are used in various cryptographic applications, such as verifying data integrity, password storage, and digital signatures.

Digital signatures, a crucial aspect of cryptographic systems, provide a means of verifying the authenticity and integrity of digital documents and messages. A digital signature is generated using the private key of a user or entity and can be verified by anyone with access to the corresponding public key. This process ensures that the signed data has not been tampered with and was indeed created by the holder of the private key.

In the realm of cryptography, randomness is highly valued. Cryptographic protocols often require the generation of random values or keys, and the quality of this randomness is essential to security. Pseudorandom number generators (PRNGs) are algorithms used to generate sequences of numbers that appear random but are generated deterministically from an initial value known as a seed.

Security in cryptography extends beyond data encryption and digital signatures; it also encompasses secure key storage. Hardware security modules (HSMs) are physical devices that provide secure key storage, key management, and cryptographic operations. HSMs are used to protect cryptographic keys from unauthorized access and tampering, making them a crucial component of many security-critical systems.

Cryptographic systems are often implemented in software libraries, and their correct operation relies on the security of the underlying software and hardware. Vulnerabilities in software implementations can lead to security breaches. Regular updates, vulnerability assessments, and best practices in software development are essential to maintaining a secure cryptographic environment.

In summary, cryptographic terminology and concepts are the building blocks of secure communication and data protection in the digital age. Understanding these concepts is essential for anyone involved in designing, implementing, or using cryptographic systems. As we continue our exploration of cryptography, we will delve deeper into specific cryptographic techniques, protocols, and applications, uncovering the intricacies that make this field both fascinating and vital to our digital world.

Chapter 2: Historical Foundations

As we journey through the fascinating history of cryptography, we find ourselves immersed in the realm of early methods and techniques employed to safeguard sensitive information. These ancient cryptographic methods may seem rudimentary by today's standards, but they laid the foundation for the sophisticated cryptographic systems we use today.

One of the earliest known methods of encryption is known as the Caesar cipher, named after Julius Caesar, the famed Roman military leader and statesman. In this cipher, each letter in the plaintext is shifted a fixed number of positions down or up the alphabet. For example, with a shift of three positions, 'A' becomes 'D,' 'B' becomes 'E,' and so on. Caesar used this technique to protect sensitive military messages from falling into the wrong hands.

Another ancient encryption technique is the substitution cipher, which goes beyond simple letter shifts. Substitution ciphers replace each letter in the plaintext with a different letter or symbol. This method introduces a level of complexity by creating a unique mapping for each character in the alphabet. While more secure than Caesar ciphers, substitution ciphers were still vulnerable to decryption through frequency analysis.

Frequency analysis is a powerful tool for cryptanalysis that dates back centuries. It exploits the fact that in any given language, certain letters and combinations of letters appear more frequently than others. For example, in English, 'E' is the most common letter. By analyzing the frequency of characters in ciphertext, cryptanalysts could make educated guesses about the corresponding letters in the plaintext.

The historical importance of cryptography is evident in the role it played during times of war and diplomacy. The Spartan military, for instance, used a device called the scytale to encrypt their messages. The scytale was a cylindrical rod around which a strip of leather or parchment was wrapped. The message was written lengthwise on the strip and then unwrapped, rendering it unreadable without the original scytale.

Throughout the ages, various civilizations developed their cryptographic methods to protect their secrets. The ancient Egyptians, for example, used hieroglyphs and other symbols to encode information. Similarly, the Greeks employed various cipher systems to encode sensitive communications. Cryptography, in many cases, became a matter of life and death during times of conflict.

In the Middle Ages, cryptography continued to evolve. One notable figure in the history of cryptography is Leon Battista Alberti, an Italian Renaissance mathematician and philosopher. In the late 15th century, Alberti devised a cipher disk, known as the Alberti cipher, which allowed users to encrypt messages using a variable substitution system. This innovation added complexity and security to cryptographic methods.

The Renaissance period also saw the publication of important cryptographic works. In 1553, the Italian author Giovan Battista Bellaso wrote "La cifra del Sig. Giovan Battista Bellaso," one of the earliest known books on cryptography. Bellaso introduced the idea of using a keyword or phrase to facilitate encryption and decryption—a concept that foreshadowed later cryptographic developments.

The 16th and 17th centuries witnessed the emergence of more complex and secure cryptographic techniques. Blaise de Vigenère, a French diplomat and cryptographer, introduced the Vigenère cipher in 1586. This cipher used a keyword to perform a series of Caesar ciphers, making it significantly more resistant to frequency analysis compared to its predecessors.

During the 18th century, cryptanalysis began to gain prominence. The Prussian military officer Friedrich Kasiski, in the 1860s, made significant contributions to the field by developing methods to break Vigenère ciphers. Kasiski's work marked a shift in focus from creating cryptographic systems to the study of breaking them—a critical development in the history of cryptography.

The 19th century brought innovations in cryptography, with the advent of mechanical cryptographic devices. The most famous of these devices was the Enigma machine, used by the German military during World War II. The Enigma machine used rotors to perform complex letter substitutions, making it a formidable challenge for Allied codebreakers.

Alan Turing, a brilliant mathematician and computer scientist, played a pivotal role in the decryption of Enigma-encrypted messages. Turing's work at Bletchley Park, along with other codebreakers, resulted in the successful deciphering of Enigma-encrypted communications, providing invaluable intelligence to the Allies and significantly contributing to their victory in the war.

The post-war era marked the beginning of the electronic age of cryptography. With the advent of computers, cryptographic techniques evolved rapidly. Symmetric key ciphers, such as the Data Encryption Standard (DES), became widely used for securing data in electronic communication and storage.

Public key cryptography, a revolutionary advancement, was introduced in the 1970s by Whitfield Diffie and Martin Hellman. This cryptographic breakthrough allowed secure communication over untrusted networks by using a pair of keys—one public and one private. This approach eliminated the need for secure key exchange between parties, making secure online communication more accessible.

The modern era of cryptography is characterized by the widespread use of cryptographic algorithms and protocols to secure data in various applications, from online banking and e-commerce to secure messaging and digital signatures. As technology continues to advance, the field of cryptography faces new challenges, such as the threat of quantum computing, which has the potential to break many existing cryptographic systems.

In summary, the history of cryptography is a testament to human ingenuity and the enduring need to protect sensitive information. From ancient methods like the Caesar cipher to the sophisticated encryption techniques of today, cryptography has evolved in response to the changing demands of a digital world. As we explore the fascinating world of cryptography further, we will uncover the intricate mathematics and algorithms that underpin the security of our modern digital lives.

Exploring the historical context of cryptography reveals its profound impact on conflicts and diplomacy throughout the centuries. Cryptography, the art and science of secure communication, has often been a pivotal element in the strategies of nations and individuals. It has played a role in both concealing sensitive information and deciphering the secrets of adversaries.

Throughout history, nations and military leaders recognized the power of cryptography in maintaining the confidentiality of their communications. In ancient times, rulers and generals relied on various encryption techniques to protect military orders, strategic plans, and diplomatic correspondence from falling into the wrong hands.

One of the earliest recorded instances of cryptography in warfare dates back to ancient Greece. During the fifth century BCE, the Greeks used a device called a "scytale" to encrypt their messages. The scytale was a rod around which a strip of leather or parchment was wrapped. The message was then written lengthwise on the strip, making it unreadable without the original scytale for decryption.

The use of simple substitution ciphers, like the Caesar cipher, was another common practice in ancient cryptography. Julius Caesar himself employed such a cipher to safeguard his military communications. In this method, each letter in the plaintext is shifted a fixed number of positions down or up the alphabet, creating ciphertext that appeared gibberish without knowledge of the shift value.

As civilizations expanded and encountered rivals and adversaries, the need for secure communication grew. Cryptography became an essential tool in diplomacy, espionage, and military campaigns. In times of war, the ability to transmit orders and intelligence securely gave one side a significant advantage over the other.

During the Middle Ages, encryption techniques continued to evolve. In the 14th century, the renowned Italian writer and poet Dante Alighieri wrote about encryption in his work "Divine Comedy." His text included a simple substitution cipher, demonstrating the widespread use and understanding of cryptographic methods during this period. One of the most famous stories of cryptography's role in history comes from the time of Queen Elizabeth I of England and her spymaster, Sir Francis Walsingham. Walsingham established an elaborate intelligence network to protect England from external threats, particularly the schemes of Mary, Queen of Scots. To conceal their messages, Walsingham's agents used a variety of cryptographic techniques, including letter frequency analysis. Letter frequency analysis, a fundamental cryptanalysis technique, exploits the fact that certain letters and combinations of letters appear more frequently than others in a given language. By analyzing the frequency of characters in ciphertext, cryptanalysts could make educated guesses about the corresponding letters in the plaintext.

The development of cryptography during the Renaissance era saw the publication of important cryptographic works. In 1553, the Italian author Giovan Battista Bellaso wrote "La cifra del Sig. Giovan Battista Bellaso," one of the earliest known books on cryptography. Bellaso introduced the idea of using a keyword or phrase to facilitate encryption and decryption—a concept that would later find its way into more advanced cryptographic systems.

The use of cryptography was not limited to European powers. In the Ottoman Empire, for example, cryptographic techniques played a significant role in maintaining the secrecy of imperial decrees and sensitive diplomatic communications. The empire's cryptanalysts were skilled in breaking foreign codes and ciphers.

As the world moved into the modern era, the importance of cryptography in conflicts became increasingly evident. During World War I, both the Allied and Central Powers used cryptographic methods to protect their military communications. The famous German encryption machine, the ADFGX cipher, posed a significant challenge to Allied cryptanalysts.

World War II marked a turning point in the history of cryptography. The German military employed the Enigma machine, a complex electromechanical device, to encrypt their communications. The efforts to break Enigma-encrypted messages became one of the most significant codebreaking endeavors in history.

British cryptanalysts at Bletchley Park, including Alan Turing, made critical breakthroughs in deciphering Enigma-encrypted messages. Their work, kept secret for many years, provided the Allies with invaluable intelligence and played a vital role in the war effort.

The successful decryption of Enigma-encrypted messages demonstrated the importance of cryptanalysis and the potential power of cryptography in conflicts. It marked a shift in focus from merely using cryptographic methods to the study of breaking them—a shift that continues to influence the field of cryptography today.

The post-World War II era saw the rise of electronic computing and the development of new cryptographic techniques. With the advent of computers, encryption methods became more complex and capable of securing vast amounts of data. Symmetric key encryption, as exemplified by the Data Encryption Standard (DES), became the standard for protecting data at rest and in transit.

The Cold War era further emphasized the need for secure communication and cryptography. Both the United States and the Soviet Union invested heavily in cryptographic research and technology. Secure communication was vital not only for military operations but also for diplomatic negotiations and intelligence gathering.

The introduction of public key cryptography in the 1970s revolutionized secure communication over open networks. Whitfield Diffie and Martin Hellman's groundbreaking work laid the foundation for secure online transactions and communications, making it possible for individuals and organizations to communicate securely without the need for a shared secret key.

As technology continues to advance, cryptography remains a critical element in ensuring the security and privacy of digital communications. It plays a vital role in protecting sensitive information, from financial transactions and medical records to personal messages and confidential business communications.

In summary, the history of cryptography's role in historical conflicts is a testament to the enduring importance of secure communication. From ancient civilizations using scytales to the codebreakers of World War II and the development of modern encryption methods, cryptography has shaped the course of history and continues to play a crucial role in our interconnected world.

Chapter 3: Basic Principles of Encryption

As we venture further into the intricate world of cryptography, it's essential to grasp the fundamental concepts of encryption and decryption. These concepts serve as the bedrock of secure communication and data protection, underpinning the confidentiality and integrity of information in the digital age.

At its core, encryption is the process of transforming plaintext data into ciphertext, rendering it unreadable to anyone without the appropriate decryption key. This transformation is achieved through the use of mathematical algorithms, which manipulate the data in a way that obscures its original meaning.

The primary purpose of encryption is to ensure the confidentiality of sensitive information. When data is encrypted, even if it falls into the wrong hands or is intercepted during transmission, it remains secure and indecipherable without the knowledge of the decryption key.

Encryption algorithms, also known as ciphers, are the mathematical rules and operations that govern the transformation of plaintext into ciphertext. These algorithms vary in complexity and security, with some designed for general-purpose encryption and others tailored for specific use cases.

One of the earliest and simplest encryption methods is the Caesar cipher, named after Julius Caesar, who is believed to have used it to protect his military messages. In a Caesar cipher, each letter in the plaintext is shifted a fixed number of positions down or up the alphabet. This shift value serves as the encryption key.

For example, with a shift of three positions, the letter 'A' becomes 'D,' 'B' becomes 'E,' and so on. To decrypt the message, the recipient needs to know the same shift value and apply it in the opposite direction.

While the Caesar cipher is easy to understand and implement, it is not secure against modern cryptanalysis techniques. The simplicity of this method makes it vulnerable to frequency analysis, where the frequency of letters in the ciphertext is analyzed to deduce the shift value and, subsequently, the plaintext.

To address the limitations of simple substitution ciphers like the Caesar cipher, more complex encryption techniques were developed. These techniques introduced greater randomness and variability into the encryption process, making it more resistant to cryptanalysis.

In the realm of modern cryptography, there are two primary categories of encryption: symmetric key cryptography and asymmetric key cryptography.

Symmetric key cryptography, often referred to as secret key cryptography, is a method where the same key is used for both encryption and decryption. The encryption key, which must remain confidential between the sender and receiver, is used to transform plaintext into ciphertext. To decrypt the data, the same key is applied in the reverse process.

Symmetric key encryption is highly efficient and suitable for encrypting large volumes of data, such as files or messages. However, it poses challenges in terms of key management and distribution. The secure exchange of the encryption key between parties is crucial, as any compromise of the key would jeopardize the confidentiality of the data.

Asymmetric key cryptography, on the other hand, introduces the concept of a key pair—a public key and a private key. These keys are mathematically related, but the encryption key (public key) can be freely shared, while the decryption key (private key) remains confidential.

When someone wants to send an encrypted message to a recipient, they use the recipient's public key to encrypt it. Only the recipient, possessing the corresponding private key, can decrypt and read the message. This approach eliminates the need for secure key exchange between parties who have never met or exchanged keys before.

Public key cryptography, exemplified by algorithms like RSA (Rivest–Shamir–Adleman) and ECC (Elliptic Curve Cryptography), revolutionized secure communication over untrusted networks, such as the internet. It paved the way for secure online transactions, encrypted email communication, and digital signatures.

The use of encryption extends beyond securing the confidentiality of data. It also plays a crucial role in ensuring data integrity and authenticity.

Cryptographic hash functions are instrumental in data integrity protection. A cryptographic hash function is a one-way mathematical operation that takes an input, often of variable length, and produces a fixed-size hash value. Even a minor change in the input data results in a vastly different hash value.

Hash functions are commonly used to verify the integrity of files, messages, and data structures. When a hash value is generated for a piece of data, any subsequent changes to that data will produce a different hash value. By comparing the newly generated hash value to the original hash value, one can detect whether the data has been tampered with.

Digital signatures, another critical aspect of cryptographic systems, provide a means of verifying the authenticity and integrity of digital documents and messages. A digital signature is generated using the private key of a user or entity and can be verified by anyone with access to the corresponding public key. This process ensures that the signed data has not been tampered with and was indeed created by the holder of the private key.

Secure communication protocols, such as SSL/TLS (Secure Sockets Layer/Transport Layer Security), employ encryption to protect the confidentiality and integrity of data transmitted between web browsers and servers. These protocols ensure that sensitive information, such as login credentials and payment details, remains confidential during online transactions.

In the modern era, cryptographic techniques have become integral to various applications and industries. They play a vital role in securing financial transactions, safeguarding medical records, enabling secure messaging platforms, and protecting sensitive government communications.

The advancement of technology and the proliferation of data-driven services have elevated the importance of encryption in our daily lives. Cryptography is not only a cornerstone of cybersecurity but also a guardian of personal privacy and digital trust.

In summary, the fundamentals of encryption and decryption form the basis of secure communication and data protection in the digital age. Whether it's the confidentiality of sensitive information, the integrity of data, or the authenticity of digital signatures, cryptography is a versatile and essential tool that underpins the security of our interconnected world.

As we delve deeper into the fascinating world of cryptography, it's essential to grasp key concepts that form the foundation of this field. These concepts are integral to understanding how cryptographic systems work, how data is secured, and how sensitive information is protected in the digital age.

One of the fundamental concepts in cryptography is encryption, the process of transforming plaintext data into ciphertext. Encryption ensures that data remains confidential and secure, even if it's intercepted during transmission or accessed by unauthorized parties.

Encryption algorithms, also known as ciphers, are mathematical rules and operations that dictate how data is transformed from plaintext to ciphertext and vice versa. These algorithms vary in complexity and security, and they play a crucial role in the strength of cryptographic systems.

A key aspect of encryption is the use of cryptographic keys. These keys are essentially secret values that determine how data is encrypted and decrypted. In symmetric key cryptography, the same key is used for both encryption and decryption, while in asymmetric key cryptography, a pair of keys—one public and one private—is used to facilitate secure communication.

Symmetric key cryptography relies on the shared secret key, which must remain confidential between the sender and receiver. The simplicity of symmetric encryption makes it efficient for encrypting large volumes of data, but it also poses challenges in key management and distribution.

Asymmetric key cryptography, on the other hand, uses a pair of keys with a mathematical relationship. The public key can be freely shared and is used to encrypt data, while the private key is kept secret and is used for decryption. This approach eliminates the need for secure key exchange between parties who have never met or exchanged keys before.

Public and private keys are integral to digital signatures, another critical component of cryptographic systems. Digital signatures provide authentication and non-repudiation in digital transactions. They ensure that a digital document or message has not been altered and that it was indeed created by the holder of the private key.

Key management is an essential aspect of cryptography. It involves key generation, distribution, storage, and rotation. Secure key management ensures that keys are protected from unauthorized access and loss, as compromising keys can lead to security breaches.

In the world of cryptography, cryptanalysis is the study of breaking cryptographic systems. Cryptanalysts analyze cryptographic algorithms and attempt to find vulnerabilities or weaknesses that can be exploited to recover the plaintext from ciphertext without knowledge of the key. Cryptanalysis involves various techniques, including mathematical analysis and computational methods.

Cryptography often involves the use of cryptographic protocols. These protocols are sets of rules and procedures that dictate how cryptographic algorithms are used to achieve specific security objectives. For example, SSL/TLS (Secure Sockets Layer/Transport Layer Security) is a cryptographic protocol used to secure data transmission over the internet, ensuring the confidentiality and integrity of data exchanged between web browsers and servers.

Secure communication protocols are essential for online interactions, such as online shopping, banking, and secure messaging. They create a secure environment for sensitive activities and protect data from eavesdropping and tampering.

Cryptographic hash functions are essential tools in ensuring data integrity. These one-way mathematical functions take input data and produce a fixed-size hash value. Even a minor change in the input data results in a vastly different hash value. Hash functions are used to verify the integrity of files and messages, providing a way to detect any unauthorized alterations.

Pseudorandom number generators (PRNGs) are algorithms used to generate sequences of numbers that appear random but are generated deterministically from an initial value known as a seed. PRNGs are crucial in cryptographic applications that require random values or keys.

The advent of quantum computing has introduced new challenges to cryptography. Quantum computers have the potential to break many of the encryption methods used today, particularly those based on integer factorization and discrete logarithm problems. This has led to the development of post-quantum cryptography, which aims to provide secure alternatives resistant to quantum attacks.

In summary, these key concepts are essential to understanding the world of cryptography. Encryption, keys, algorithms, protocols, hash functions, and cryptanalysis are the building blocks of secure communication and data protection in the digital age. As technology continues to advance, cryptography remains at the forefront of safeguarding sensitive information and ensuring the security and privacy of our digital interactions.

Chapter 4: Symmetric Key Cryptography

In our exploration of cryptography, one of the fundamental concepts we encounter is symmetric key algorithms, a cornerstone of modern encryption techniques. Symmetric key algorithms, also known as secret key algorithms, form the basis of many secure communication and data protection systems. They play a crucial role in safeguarding sensitive information, ensuring confidentiality, and enabling secure data exchange.

At the heart of symmetric key cryptography lies a shared secret key, a secret piece of information that is known only to the parties involved in the communication. This shared secret key is used both for the encryption of plaintext data and the decryption of ciphertext, hence the term "symmetric."

The concept of symmetric key encryption is elegantly simple. When a sender wants to send an encrypted message to a recipient, they use the shared secret key to perform the encryption process. This process transforms the plaintext data into ciphertext, which appears as a seemingly random sequence of characters, thereby concealing its original meaning.

The recipient, possessing the same shared secret key, can then decrypt the ciphertext and recover the original plaintext. This straightforward approach to encryption and decryption is highly efficient, making symmetric key algorithms well-suited for encrypting large volumes of data, such as files, messages, and network traffic.

Symmetric key algorithms are characterized by their speed and computational efficiency, making them ideal for real-time applications where encryption and decryption must occur rapidly. These algorithms are often used to secure data at rest, such as files stored on a hard drive, and data in transit, such as network communications.

One of the simplest and historically significant symmetric key algorithms is the Caesar cipher, which dates back to ancient Rome. In the Caesar cipher, each letter in the plaintext is shifted a fixed number of positions down or up the alphabet. This shift value serves as the encryption key, and it must be known to both the sender and recipient for successful communication.

For example, with a shift of three positions, the letter 'A' becomes 'D,' 'B' becomes 'E,' and so on. To decrypt the message, the recipient applies the same shift value in the opposite direction, transforming the ciphertext back into plaintext.

While the Caesar cipher illustrates the basic concept of symmetric key encryption, it is not secure against modern cryptanalysis techniques. The simplicity of this method makes it vulnerable to frequency analysis, a technique where the frequency of letters in the ciphertext is analyzed to deduce the shift value and, consequently, the plaintext.

To address the limitations of simple substitution ciphers like the Caesar cipher, more complex symmetric key algorithms were developed. These algorithms introduced greater randomness and variability into the encryption process, making them more resistant to cryptanalysis.

One example of a more sophisticated symmetric key algorithm is the Data Encryption Standard (DES), which was widely used in the 1970s and 1980s. DES is a block cipher that operates on fixed-size blocks of data, typically 64 bits at a time. It uses a 56-bit key to perform multiple rounds of permutation and substitution to encrypt and decrypt data.

DES was considered highly secure at the time of its introduction, but as computing power increased, it became vulnerable to brute-force attacks, where an attacker systematically tries all possible keys to decrypt the data. To address this vulnerability, the Advanced Encryption Standard (AES) was developed as a replacement for DES. AES offers improved security with key lengths of 128, 192, or 256 bits and has become the de facto symmetric key algorithm for secure data encryption today.

In symmetric key cryptography, key management is a critical aspect of ensuring the security of encrypted data. Key management involves various processes, such as key generation, distribution, storage, and rotation. Proper key management is essential to protect keys from unauthorized access and loss, as compromising the key can lead to the compromise of encrypted data.

While symmetric key algorithms excel in efficiency and speed, they face challenges related to key exchange and distribution in secure communication. In many cases, the sender and recipient must securely share the secret key before they can communicate securely. This requirement raises questions about the secure transmission of keys, particularly in scenarios where the parties have never met or exchanged keys before.

The Diffie-Hellman key exchange, a cryptographic protocol developed in the late 1970s, addresses the challenge of secure key exchange in symmetric key cryptography. Diffie-Hellman allows two parties to agree on a shared secret key over an insecure communication channel without revealing the key itself. This protocol laid the foundation for secure key exchange in various cryptographic systems.

In the world of modern symmetric key algorithms, confidentiality is not the only consideration. Data integrity, ensuring that data has not been tampered with during transmission or storage, is equally important. Cryptographic hash functions are instrumental in verifying data integrity.

A cryptographic hash function is a one-way mathematical operation that takes an input, often of variable length, and produces a fixed-size hash value. Even a minor change in the input data results in a vastly different hash value. Hash functions are used to generate checksums and digital signatures, providing a means to verify the integrity of files, messages, and data structures.

In summary, symmetric key algorithms are a fundamental component of cryptography, offering efficient and secure methods for data encryption and decryption. The shared secret key is central to their operation, and key management is essential to their security. As technology continues to advance, symmetric key algorithms remain a reliable choice for safeguarding data in various applications, from secure communications to data protection at rest.

In our ongoing exploration of cryptography, we delve deeper into the concept of achieving data confidentiality, a fundamental goal in secure communication and data protection. One of the key techniques employed to achieve data confidentiality is symmetric encryption, which we have previously discussed as a cornerstone of modern encryption methods.

The primary aim of symmetric encryption is to ensure that sensitive data remains confidential and secure, particularly during transmission or when stored on various devices or servers. Data confidentiality is paramount when dealing with personal information, financial transactions, medical records, and any other type of sensitive data that should not be accessible to unauthorized individuals or entities.

Symmetric encryption relies on a shared secret key, which is known only to the parties involved in the communication or data exchange. This shared secret key serves as the linchpin of confidentiality, as it is used both for the encryption of plaintext data and the decryption of ciphertext, rendering the data secure from prying eyes.

The encryption process is designed to transform plaintext data into ciphertext in such a way that the original content is obscured and can only be revealed through decryption with the same shared secret key. This process involves mathematical algorithms that manipulate the data, making it appear as an unintelligible sequence of characters to anyone without access to the key.

When data is encrypted using a symmetric key algorithm, it becomes resistant to unauthorized access and eavesdropping. Even if an attacker intercepts the encrypted data, they would need knowledge of the shared secret key to decrypt it and gain access to the original content. This level of security is what makes symmetric encryption a fundamental tool for data confidentiality.

One of the strengths of symmetric encryption is its efficiency and speed. The encryption and decryption processes are relatively fast, making it suitable for real-time applications where data needs to be secured quickly, such as in secure messaging, online banking, and e-commerce transactions.

Symmetric encryption algorithms come in various flavors, with different levels of complexity and security. The choice of algorithm depends on the specific use case and the required level of security. Some well-known symmetric encryption algorithms include the Data Encryption Standard (DES), the Advanced Encryption Standard (AES), and the Triple Data Encryption Algorithm (3DES), among others.

AES, in particular, has become the de facto standard for symmetric key encryption due to its robust security and efficiency. AES offers different key lengths, including 128, 192, and 256 bits, allowing organizations to choose the appropriate level of security for their applications.

To ensure the confidentiality of data, it is crucial to manage the symmetric encryption keys effectively. Key management encompasses processes such as key generation, distribution, storage, and rotation. Proper key management is essential to protect keys from unauthorized access, loss, or compromise, as any breach of the key can lead to a breach of the encrypted data.

One of the challenges in symmetric encryption is the secure exchange of encryption keys between the parties involved. If an attacker intercepts the shared secret key during key exchange, they can potentially decrypt all future communications. To address this challenge, secure key exchange protocols, such as the Diffie-Hellman key exchange, have been developed to enable parties to agree on a shared secret key over an insecure communication channel without revealing the key itself.

While symmetric encryption excels in data confidentiality, it faces challenges in scenarios where parties have never met or exchanged keys before. In these cases, asymmetric key cryptography, which relies on a pair of keys—a public key and a private key—provides a solution.

In asymmetric key cryptography, the public key is freely shared and can be used to encrypt data, while the private key, kept secret, is used for decryption. This approach eliminates the need for the secure exchange of symmetric keys between parties who have not established prior trust.

Public key cryptography, often referred to as asymmetric encryption, complements symmetric encryption and is commonly used for secure key exchange in scenarios like secure email communication and SSL/TLS (Secure Sockets Layer/Transport Layer Security) for secure web browsing.

Data confidentiality in symmetric encryption is not limited to protecting data in transit; it is equally essential for safeguarding data at rest. When data is stored on devices or servers, it can be vulnerable to unauthorized access, theft, or breaches. Symmetric encryption ensures that even if an attacker gains physical or digital access to the storage medium, they cannot read the data without the shared secret key.

This aspect of data confidentiality is crucial in scenarios like securing files on a hard drive, encrypting data backups, and protecting sensitive databases. By encrypting data at rest, organizations can mitigate the risk of data breaches and ensure that sensitive information remains confidential, even in the event of a security incident.

Cryptographic hash functions also play a role in ensuring data confidentiality. While their primary purpose is to verify data integrity, they indirectly contribute to data confidentiality by making it extremely difficult for attackers to reverse-engineer the original data from the hash value.

A cryptographic hash function takes an input, often of variable length, and produces a fixed-size hash value. Even a minor change in the input data results in a vastly different hash value. This one-way operation ensures that the original data cannot be easily reconstructed from the hash.

By using cryptographic hash functions, organizations can protect sensitive data, such as passwords, stored in databases. Instead of storing plaintext passwords, which would be vulnerable if the database were compromised, organizations can store the hash values of passwords. When users log in, their entered passwords are hashed and compared to the stored hash values, providing an additional layer of data confidentiality.

In summary, achieving data confidentiality is a central objective in the field of cryptography, and symmetric encryption is a powerful tool for securing sensitive information. With its efficiency, speed, and robust security, symmetric encryption ensures that data remains confidential both in transit and at rest. As technology continues to evolve, the importance of data confidentiality remains paramount in our interconnected world.

Chapter 5: Public Key Cryptography

In our journey through the intricate world of cryptography, we come across a revolutionary concept: public key cryptography. This innovation has transformed the way we secure digital communications and laid the foundation for many of the secure online transactions and communications we rely on today.

Public key cryptography, also known as asymmetric key cryptography, introduces a novel approach to secure communication. Unlike symmetric key cryptography, where a single shared secret key is used for both encryption and decryption, public key cryptography employs a pair of keys—a public key and a private key.

The public key, as its name suggests, is made available to anyone who wants to communicate securely with the key holder. This key is used to encrypt data before it is sent to the key holder. Importantly, while the public key can be used for encryption, it cannot be used to decrypt the data once it has been encrypted.

On the other hand, the private key remains confidential and is known only to the key holder. This private key is used to decrypt data that has been encrypted with the corresponding public key. This key pair, consisting of a public key and a private key, forms the basis of public key cryptography and enables secure communication between parties that have never met or exchanged keys before.

One of the earliest pioneers of public key cryptography was Whitfield Diffie, who, along with Martin Hellman, introduced the concept in their groundbreaking 1976 paper titled "New Directions in Cryptography." This paper laid the theoretical foundation for secure key exchange without the need for a shared secret key.

In the traditional model of symmetric key cryptography, secure communication between two parties required them to both possess the same shared secret key. However, Diffie and Hellman's innovation changed this paradigm. With public key cryptography, two parties can communicate securely without the need for prior key exchange.

The Diffie-Hellman key exchange, one of the first practical implementations of public key cryptography, allows two parties to agree on a shared secret key over an insecure communication channel without revealing the key itself. This protocol marked a significant shift in the field of cryptography and opened up new possibilities for secure digital communication.

Another milestone in the development of public key cryptography was the introduction of the RSA algorithm, named after its inventors, Ron Rivest, Adi Shamir, and Leonard Adleman, in 1977. RSA stands for Rivest-Shamir-Adleman and is one of the most widely used public key encryption algorithms today.

The RSA algorithm is based on the mathematical properties of large prime numbers and their factorization. It relies on the difficulty of factoring the product of two large prime numbers to derive the private key from the public key. This complexity forms the foundation of RSA's security.

RSA encryption allows anyone to encrypt data using the recipient's public key, ensuring confidentiality during data transmission. Only the recipient, who possesses the corresponding private key, can decrypt the data and access the original content. This approach provides a secure means of communication over open networks, such as the internet.

Public key cryptography has found numerous applications in secure digital communication. One of the most notable uses is in secure email communication. When you send an encrypted email, your email client uses the recipient's public key to encrypt the message. Only the recipient, with the corresponding private key, can decrypt and read the email. This ensures the confidentiality of your message, protecting it from unauthorized access during transmission.

Secure online transactions also rely heavily on public key cryptography. When you make a purchase online or log in to your bank's website, secure communication protocols like SSL/TLS (Secure Sockets Layer/Transport Layer Security) use public key cryptography to establish secure connections between your browser and the server. This ensures that your financial information and login credentials are transmitted securely and cannot be intercepted by malicious actors.

Digital signatures, another crucial application of public key cryptography, provide a means of verifying the authenticity and integrity of digital documents and messages. A digital signature is created using the private key of the sender and can be verified by anyone with access to the sender's public key. This process ensures that the signed data has not been tampered with and was indeed created by the holder of the private key.

The advent of blockchain technology and cryptocurrencies has also harnessed the power of public key cryptography. Blockchain, the underlying technology of cryptocurrencies like Bitcoin, relies on digital signatures generated using public and private key pairs. These digital signatures verify transactions and ensure the integrity of the blockchain ledger.

Public key cryptography has made secure communication and transactions accessible to a wide range of users, from individuals sending encrypted emails to businesses conducting secure online commerce. Its versatility and effectiveness have transformed the way we interact digitally, enabling trust and privacy in an interconnected world.

As with any technological advancement, public key cryptography has also faced challenges and threats. The rise of quantum computing, with its potential to break many of the encryption methods used today, has prompted the development of post-quantum cryptography. Post-quantum cryptography aims to provide secure alternatives that are resistant to quantum attacks.

In summary, the innovation of public key cryptography has revolutionized the way we secure digital communication and transactions. The concept of using a pair of keys—one public and one private—has empowered individuals and organizations to communicate securely over untrusted networks, protect their data, and verify the authenticity of digital documents. As technology continues to evolve, public key cryptography remains an essential tool for ensuring the security and privacy of our digital interactions.

In our ongoing exploration of cryptography, we delve deeper into the topic of digital signatures and the essential role they play in ensuring the authenticity and integrity of digital documents and messages. Digital signatures provide a powerful means of verifying the origin and integrity of data in the digital age, offering a secure way to assert the authorship of documents, confirm the validity of transactions, and establish trust in electronic communications.

At its core, a digital signature is a cryptographic technique that allows a sender to sign a piece of digital content, such as an email, a contract, or a software update. This digital signature serves as a unique identifier, akin to a handwritten signature in the physical world, but with the added benefit of being mathematically secure and tamper-evident.

To create a digital signature, the sender uses their private key to perform a mathematical operation on the content they wish to sign. This operation generates a unique signature value that is specific to both the content and the private key. This signature value is then appended to the digital content, creating a signed document.

Importantly, the digital signature process also includes a hashing step. A cryptographic hash function is applied to the content before signing it. This hash value is what is actually signed, not the entire content. Hashing ensures that the digital signature remains of manageable size and that it's computationally efficient to verify.

Once a digital document with a signature is received, the recipient can use the sender's public key to verify the authenticity and integrity of the document. By applying the sender's public key to the digital signature, the recipient can check whether the signature corresponds to the content and whether the content has been altered in transit.

If the recipient's verification process succeeds, it confirms that the document was indeed signed by the sender and that the content has not been tampered with. This verification process provides assurance that the document is authentic and trustworthy.

One of the key advantages of digital signatures is the concept of non-repudiation. Non-repudiation means that the sender cannot deny their involvement in creating and signing the document. Since the digital signature is uniquely tied to the sender's private key, it is computationally infeasible for anyone else to create a valid signature that matches both the content and the sender's key.

This feature makes digital signatures invaluable in legal and contractual contexts, where the authenticity of documents and agreements is paramount. Courts and regulatory bodies often accept digitally signed documents as legally binding, as they provide a high level of confidence in the identity of the signatory and the integrity of the document.

The use of digital signatures extends to various domains and industries. In the realm of secure email communication, digital signatures enable users to sign their emails, proving the authenticity of the sender and ensuring that the content has not been altered during transmission. This is particularly important in business communications and in verifying the source of sensitive information.

Digital signatures also play a central role in secure online transactions. When you make an online purchase, your payment information is often digitally signed by the payment processor or financial institution, ensuring the security and authenticity of the transaction. This is crucial for building trust in e-commerce and financial services.

In the context of software distribution and updates, digital signatures are used to verify the authenticity and integrity of software packages. When you download software from a trusted source, a digital signature accompanying the software package assures you that it has not been tampered with and that it originates from the legitimate software provider.

Furthermore, digital signatures are a key component of public key infrastructure (PKI), a framework that provides a secure and scalable way to manage digital certificates, which are the digital counterparts of traditional ID cards or passports. Digital certificates bind an individual's identity to their public key and are issued by trusted entities called certificate authorities (CAs).

In a PKI, CAs are responsible for verifying the identity of certificate holders and issuing digital certificates that attest to their identity. These certificates are digitally signed by the CA, adding an extra layer of trust. Users or organizations can then present these certificates to prove their identity in online interactions.

For example, when you visit a secure website that uses the HTTPS protocol, your browser verifies the authenticity of the website's digital certificate, which has been issued by a trusted CA. This verification process ensures that you are indeed connecting to the legitimate website and not to an impostor.

Digital signatures also play a role in protecting the integrity of software updates. When you receive a software update for your operating system or applications, the digital signature on the update file confirms that it has not been tampered with and that it comes from the legitimate software vendor.

In the world of blockchain technology, digital signatures are an integral part of the consensus mechanism. Blockchain networks rely on cryptographic signatures to verify the authenticity and integrity of transactions added to the ledger. These signatures are generated using the private keys of participants and are used to confirm ownership and authorization for transactions.

In summary, digital signatures are a vital component of modern cryptographic systems, offering a secure means of verifying the authenticity and integrity of digital documents and messages. They provide non-repudiation, making it difficult for senders to deny their involvement, and they have wide-ranging applications in secure email communication, online transactions, software distribution, and public key infrastructure. Digital signatures are essential tools for establishing trust and security in the digital world.

Chapter 6: Key Management and Distribution

In the realm of cryptography, one of the foundational aspects that underpin security is the generation of secure cryptographic keys. Secure key generation is a critical step in ensuring the confidentiality, integrity, and authenticity of data in cryptographic systems. In this chapter, we will explore various strategies and techniques for generating cryptographic keys that can withstand the relentless efforts of adversaries seeking to compromise security.

First and foremost, the security of any cryptographic system begins with the generation of truly random numbers. Randomness is essential because predictable keys are vulnerable to attacks. Cryptographic keys must be unpredictable and generated in such a way that they cannot be easily guessed or deduced by attackers.

Pseudo-random number generators (PRNGs) are commonly used to generate cryptographic keys. PRNGs produce sequences of numbers that appear random but are generated algorithmically from an initial seed value. However, the security of PRNGs depends on the quality of the underlying algorithm and the entropy of the seed value.

To enhance the randomness and security of keys, cryptographic systems often rely on a combination of entropy sources. Entropy sources are inputs that provide a degree of unpredictability. These sources may include environmental factors such as mouse movements, keyboard presses, system events, or hardware-based sources like electronic noise in semiconductors.

In practice, the collection of entropy from various sources is referred to as "entropy gathering." The gathered entropy is then processed and used to seed a PRNG, ensuring that the resulting keys are more robust against predictive attacks.

Hardware security modules (HSMs) are specialized devices designed to enhance key generation security. HSMs contain dedicated hardware for generating, storing, and managing cryptographic keys. They often have physical tamper protection mechanisms to safeguard keys against unauthorized access or theft.

One common approach to secure key generation is to use a cryptographically secure pseudorandom number generator (CSPRNG). CSPRNGs are designed with cryptographic properties that make it computationally infeasible for an attacker to predict future numbers in the sequence, even if they know some of the previous numbers.

Another strategy for secure key generation is to use true random number generators (TRNGs). TRNGs derive randomness from physical processes that are inherently unpredictable, such as electronic noise, radioactive decay, or atmospheric noise. TRNGs provide a higher level of security as they are not based on algorithms and are less susceptible to predictable patterns.

To further enhance key generation security, cryptographic standards and protocols often specify key lengths and generation methods that align with the level of security required for a particular application. For example, the Advanced Encryption Standard (AES) specifies key lengths of 128, 192, and 256 bits, with longer keys providing stronger security.

Randomness testing is a crucial step in assessing the quality of generated cryptographic keys. Various statistical tests and methods are employed to evaluate the randomness of keys and to ensure that they meet the required cryptographic standards. These tests help detect any bias or patterns that might compromise key security.

Cryptographic key generation must also consider key management, which involves securely storing and distributing keys. Keys must be protected from unauthorized access and potential breaches. Key management practices include secure key storage, secure key exchange protocols, and key rotation strategies.

In the context of public key cryptography, key pairs consist of a public key and a private key. The security of the system relies on the secrecy of the private key. Therefore, generating and safeguarding the private key is of utmost importance. Secure key generation for public key cryptography typically involves using strong pseudorandom number generators and careful management of the private key.

In many cryptographic systems, key generation is a one-time event, and the generated keys are used repeatedly for encryption and decryption. As a result, key generation must be conducted with the utmost care, as any compromise in the generation process can have far-reaching consequences for the security of the system.

In secure key generation, the principle of key diversification is often applied. Key diversification involves generating different keys for different purposes or sessions. This approach limits the impact of a compromised key, as it only affects a specific context or session.

Cryptographic agility is another important consideration in secure key generation. It refers to the ability to change cryptographic keys and algorithms when necessary to adapt to evolving security threats. Cryptographic agility allows systems to transition to stronger keys and algorithms as vulnerabilities are discovered in older ones.

In summary, secure key generation is a foundational element in the field of cryptography. It involves the generation of cryptographic keys that are truly random, unpredictable, and resistant to attacks. Various strategies, including the use of cryptographic pseudorandom number generators, entropy sources, and hardware security modules, contribute to the generation of secure keys. Key management practices, randomness testing, and cryptographic agility further enhance the security of cryptographic systems. By carefully considering these strategies and best practices, cryptographic systems can maintain the confidentiality, integrity, and authenticity of data in the face of determined adversaries.

In the intricate world of cryptography, one of the most challenging aspects is securely distributing cryptographic keys to ensure the confidentiality, integrity, and authenticity of communications. Key distribution protocols are the mechanisms and strategies employed to securely transmit cryptographic keys between parties involved in a secure communication.

The fundamental problem in key distribution is that two parties wishing to communicate securely must share a secret key that can be used for encryption and decryption. However, the challenge lies in exchanging this secret key without it being intercepted by potential adversaries.

One of the earliest and simplest key distribution methods is the use of physical key exchange. In this approach, two parties meet in person and exchange physical keys, such as USB tokens or smartcards, that contain the shared secret key. While this method is secure, it is not practical for many scenarios, especially in today's globally connected world.

To address the limitations of physical key exchange, key distribution protocols rely on mathematical techniques and cryptographic algorithms to securely transmit keys over untrusted communication channels. These protocols are designed to prevent eavesdroppers from intercepting the keys and to provide a high level of assurance that the keys remain confidential.

One widely used key distribution protocol is the Diffie-Hellman key exchange, which was introduced in 1976. The Diffie-Hellman protocol enables two parties to agree on a shared secret key over an insecure communication channel without revealing the key itself. The security of this protocol is based on the difficulty of the discrete logarithm problem, making it computationally infeasible for attackers to deduce the shared secret key from the exchanged values.

The Diffie-Hellman key exchange begins with both parties agreeing on two publicly known values: a large prime number and a generator value. Each party then independently selects a private key and performs mathematical operations to derive a public key. The public keys are exchanged, and each party uses its private key and the received public key to compute a shared secret key.

One of the advantages of the Diffie-Hellman key exchange is that even if an attacker intercepts the public keys exchanged during the process, they cannot compute the shared secret key without knowledge of the private keys. This property ensures the confidentiality of the key exchange.

Another widely used key distribution protocol is the RSA key exchange, which is based on the RSA algorithm introduced in the late 1970s. RSA key exchange relies on the mathematical properties of large prime numbers and their factorization. In RSA, each party generates a key pair consisting of a public key and a private key.

The sender encrypts the shared secret key with the recipient's public key and sends the encrypted key to the recipient. The recipient, possessing the corresponding private key, can decrypt the message and obtain the shared secret key. RSA key exchange provides confidentiality and authentication, as the recipient can be assured that the sender possesses the private key corresponding to the public key used for encryption.

While the Diffie-Hellman and RSA key exchange protocols have been widely adopted, they are not without their challenges. One significant challenge is the security of the public keys themselves. If an attacker can substitute a public key with their own, they can intercept and manipulate the key exchange.

To address this issue, public key infrastructure (PKI) systems have been developed to provide a framework for securely managing and distributing public keys. PKI involves the use of certificate authorities (CAs) that verify the identity of individuals and organizations and issue digital certificates that bind a public key to an identity.

Digital certificates issued by CAs serve as a trust anchor for public keys. They are signed by the CA, adding an additional layer of authentication and ensuring that the public key has not been tampered with. When parties exchange public keys, they can verify the authenticity of the keys by checking the digital certificates provided by the CAs.

However, PKI also faces challenges related to the trustworthiness of CAs and the potential for certificate revocation in the event of compromised private keys. Organizations must carefully manage their certificates and rely on trusted CAs to maintain the integrity of the PKI.

Another challenge in key distribution is the use of symmetric key encryption to protect the confidentiality of keys during transmission. While symmetric key encryption provides strong security, it introduces the need to securely exchange an initial symmetric key, often referred to as a session key, before symmetric encryption can be used for subsequent communications.

This initial key exchange can be vulnerable to attacks if not properly protected. Key distribution protocols often employ asymmetric key encryption, such as RSA, to securely exchange the initial session key. Once the session key is established, symmetric encryption is used for the actual data communication, which is more efficient than asymmetric encryption for large amounts of data.

In addition to the challenges mentioned, key distribution protocols must also consider key management practices, including key expiration, key rotation, and key storage. Effective key management is essential to protect keys from unauthorized access, loss, or compromise, as any breach of the key can lead to a breach of the encrypted data.

In summary, key distribution protocols are a critical component of secure communication in the field of cryptography. These protocols address the challenge of securely transmitting cryptographic keys over untrusted communication channels. While protocols like Diffie-Hellman and RSA key exchange provide strong security, they also require careful consideration of key management, public key infrastructure, and the protection of initial session keys. By addressing these challenges, cryptographic systems can ensure the confidentiality, integrity, and authenticity of their communications.

Chapter 7: Cryptographic Applications in Everyday Life

In today's interconnected world, messaging and communication apps have become an integral part of our daily lives, facilitating instant communication and information sharing across the globe. These apps have transformed the way we interact, enabling us to connect with friends, family, colleagues, and even strangers with unprecedented ease and speed.

However, with the convenience of messaging and communication apps comes the critical concern of security and privacy. The exchange of personal messages, sensitive information, and confidential data through these platforms requires robust protection to ensure that our communications remain private and secure from prying eyes and malicious actors.

This is where encryption plays a pivotal role. Encryption is the process of converting plain text messages or data into a scrambled form that can only be deciphered by someone who possesses the decryption key. In the context of messaging and communication apps, encryption is employed to safeguard the content of our messages from unauthorized access.

End-to-end encryption is a key concept in securing messaging apps. This form of encryption ensures that only the sender and the intended recipient of a message can decrypt and read its contents. Even the service provider facilitating the communication cannot access the message in its decrypted form. End-to-end encryption guarantees that the messages remain private and confidential, even if they traverse through servers or networks owned by the app provider.

One of the most well-known implementations of end-to-end encryption is the Signal Protocol. Signal, a privacy-focused messaging app, employs this protocol to secure the communications of its users. When two Signal users exchange messages, the content is encrypted on the sender's device using a symmetric encryption key. This key is generated for that specific message and is known only to the sender and the recipient.

The encrypted message is transmitted to the recipient's device, where it can only be decrypted using the shared encryption key. Importantly, this decryption key is never transmitted over the network or stored on the service provider's servers, ensuring that even the provider cannot access the message.

WhatsApp, another widely used messaging app, also employs end-to-end encryption powered by the Signal Protocol. This encryption has become a hallmark of WhatsApp's commitment to user privacy. When you send a message on WhatsApp, it is encrypted on your device before being sent to the recipient. Only the recipient's device possesses the necessary decryption key to read the message.

Telegram, another popular messaging app, offers a feature called "Secret Chats," which uses a similar end-to-end encryption mechanism. In a Secret Chat, the messages are encrypted on both the sender's and recipient's devices, making them inaccessible to anyone else, including the app's servers.

Secure key exchange is a critical component of end-to-end encryption. To ensure that only the intended recipient can decrypt a message, the sender and recipient must exchange encryption keys securely. This is typically accomplished through a process called "key exchange," where both parties agree on a shared encryption key without revealing it to anyone else.

In some cases, users may opt to verify each other's identity by comparing a security code or fingerprint. This verification step ensures that the keys exchanged belong to the intended recipients and have not been tampered with by a malicious actor.

While end-to-end encryption provides a high level of security and privacy, it also introduces challenges. One such challenge is the inability of service providers to access message content even when requested for legal or security reasons. This tension between user privacy and law enforcement access to communications has sparked debates and discussions worldwide.

In response to these challenges, some messaging apps have implemented additional features that balance security with user convenience. For example, Apple's iMessage employs end-to-end encryption, but it also allows users to back up their messages to iCloud. While these backups are encrypted, Apple retains the ability to decrypt them if required by law enforcement or for account recovery purposes.

The balance between user privacy and access for legitimate reasons is a complex issue, and it varies from one messaging app to another. It reflects the broader debate about the role of encryption in the digital age and the competing interests of privacy, security, and law enforcement.

It's essential for users to be aware of the encryption methods employed by the messaging apps they use and to make informed choices based on their privacy and security preferences. Some apps prioritize privacy and security above all else, while others may offer additional features at the expense of some degree of encryption.

In summary, encryption is a fundamental component of messaging and communication apps, playing a crucial role in safeguarding the privacy and security of our digital communications. End-to-end encryption ensures that only the sender and recipient of a message can decrypt and read its contents, protecting it from unauthorized access. While encryption enhances user privacy, it also presents challenges related to lawful access and the balance between security and convenience. As users, understanding the encryption methods employed by our chosen messaging apps empowers us to make informed decisions about our digital privacy.

In the fast-paced world of e-commerce, where transactions happen at the speed of a click, security is paramount. Consumers and businesses alike rely on the internet for buying and selling products and services, making online security a critical concern. Cryptographic solutions play a central role in ensuring the security and integrity of e-commerce transactions, enabling safe and trustworthy online interactions.

One of the primary challenges in e-commerce is protecting sensitive information, such as credit card numbers, personal details, and financial data, from falling into the wrong hands. Cryptography offers a robust defense mechanism against data breaches and cyberattacks, allowing confidential information to be transmitted and stored securely.

Secure Sockets Layer (SSL) and its successor, Transport Layer Security (TLS), are cryptographic protocols that establish secure connections over the internet. When you see a padlock icon or "https://" in your browser's address bar, it indicates that SSL or TLS is in use, encrypting the data exchanged between your device and the e-commerce website.

These protocols ensure that the data transmitted during an online purchase, including your payment information, is encrypted before leaving your device and decrypted only on the e-commerce server. Even if intercepted by a malicious actor during transmission, the encrypted data remains indecipherable without the encryption key.

Public Key Infrastructure (PKI) is another cryptographic solution that underpins e-commerce security. PKI enables the use of digital certificates to verify the authenticity of websites and the encryption of data. Certificate authorities (CAs) issue digital certificates, which serve as a kind of online identity card for websites. When you visit an e-commerce site with a valid digital certificate, your browser checks the certificate's authenticity, ensuring that you are indeed connecting to the legitimate website and not a malicious imitation.

Digital certificates are essential for establishing trust between customers and e-commerce platforms. They provide assurance that the website is who it claims to be, reducing the risk of phishing attacks and fraudulent websites attempting to steal sensitive information.

In the realm of online payment security, cryptographic tokens play a crucial role. Tokenization involves replacing sensitive data, such as credit card numbers, with a unique token that has no intrinsic value and cannot be used for unauthorized transactions. When you make an online purchase, your payment information is tokenized, ensuring that even if a cybercriminal gains access to the token, they cannot use it to make fraudulent transactions.

Cryptographic algorithms like Advanced Encryption Standard (AES) are employed in tokenization to ensure that the tokens remain secure and resistant to decryption. Tokenization enhances the security of e-commerce transactions and reduces the risk of data breaches that can occur when sensitive payment data is stored by merchants.

Multi-factor authentication (MFA) is another cryptographic security measure that adds an extra layer of protection to e-commerce transactions. MFA requires users to provide two or more authentication factors before gaining access to their accounts or authorizing a transaction. One of these factors is often something the user knows, like a password, while another factor may be something they have, such as a mobile device or a hardware token.

MFA enhances e-commerce security by making it significantly more challenging for unauthorized individuals to gain access to accounts or conduct fraudulent transactions. Even if a cybercriminal obtains a user's password, they would still need the additional authentication factors to proceed.

In addition to securing transactions, cryptography also plays a role in protecting the integrity of e-commerce data. Digital signatures, a cryptographic technique, can be used to verify the authenticity of digital documents, contracts, and receipts in e-commerce transactions. When a document is digitally signed, it ensures that the document has not been altered since the signature was applied, adding an extra layer of trust to online agreements.

Cryptographic hashing is employed to create unique, fixed-length representations of data, known as hash values or message digests. These hash values can be used to verify the integrity of files and data exchanged in e-commerce. By comparing the hash value of a received file with a previously calculated hash value, users can confirm whether the file has been tampered with during transmission.

Blockchain technology, often associated with cryptocurrencies, has also found its way into e-commerce security. Blockchain employs cryptographic algorithms to create immutable and transparent ledgers of transactions. In e-commerce, this technology can be used to track the provenance of products, ensuring the authenticity of goods and reducing the risk of counterfeits.

Moreover, blockchain-based smart contracts enable automated, secure, and transparent execution of agreements in e-commerce. These self-executing contracts are tamper-proof and automatically enforce the terms and conditions specified in the contract code, providing an additional layer of trust and security for e-commerce transactions.

While cryptographic solutions are instrumental in enhancing e-commerce security, it's essential for both businesses and consumers to remain vigilant and stay informed about emerging threats and best practices. Cybersecurity is an ever-evolving field, and staying up-to-date with the latest developments is crucial for safeguarding e-commerce transactions and data.

In summary, cryptographic solutions are indispensable for ensuring the security, integrity, and trustworthiness of e-commerce transactions. Technologies such as SSL/TLS, PKI, tokenization, multi-factor authentication, digital signatures, and blockchain play pivotal roles in safeguarding sensitive information and preventing data breaches. As the e-commerce landscape continues to evolve, the effective use of cryptography remains a cornerstone of online security for businesses and consumers alike.

Chapter 8: Cryptographic Security and Threats

In the ever-evolving landscape of cryptography and cybersecurity, it's crucial to be aware of common cryptographic vulnerabilities that can potentially compromise the security of systems and data. These vulnerabilities represent weaknesses in cryptographic implementations and practices, which can be exploited by malicious actors to breach security measures and gain unauthorized access to sensitive information.

One common cryptographic vulnerability is weak key management. Weak key management occurs when cryptographic keys are not generated, stored, or handled securely. Inadequate key generation methods or the use of easily guessable keys can lead to the compromise of encrypted data. Proper key management practices, such as using strong random key generation and protecting keys from unauthorized access, are essential to mitigate this vulnerability.

Another vulnerability is algorithmic weaknesses. Over time, cryptographic algorithms can become vulnerable to attacks as computing power increases and new mathematical techniques are developed. For example, older encryption algorithms like DES (Data Encryption Standard) have been replaced with stronger alternatives due to advances in cryptanalysis. It's crucial to stay up-to-date with the latest cryptographic standards and best practices to avoid using deprecated or vulnerable algorithms.

Cryptographic protocols can also introduce vulnerabilities if not implemented correctly. A classic example is the padding oracle attack, which targets the way encrypted data is padded before encryption. If an attacker can manipulate the padding and observe how the server responds, they may gain insights into the encrypted content. Implementing protocols securely and following recommended guidelines is essential to prevent such vulnerabilities.

Side-channel attacks are another category of vulnerabilities. These attacks exploit information leaked through unintended channels, such as power consumption, electromagnetic radiation, or execution time. By analyzing these side-channel leaks, attackers can deduce cryptographic keys or sensitive data. Protecting against side-channel attacks requires careful engineering of cryptographic implementations and the use of countermeasures like constant-time algorithms.

A well-known vulnerability in cryptographic systems is the use of weak or predictable initialization vectors (IVs) in encryption algorithms. IVs are used to ensure that the same plaintext encrypted with the same key results in different ciphertexts. When weak or predictable IVs are used, it becomes easier for attackers to deduce patterns in encrypted data, potentially leading to the recovery of the key or plaintext.

Cryptographic vulnerabilities can also arise from improper random number generation. Truly random and unpredictable values are essential for cryptographic keys and nonces. If a random number generator is flawed or poorly implemented, it can lead to the generation of weak keys or predictable values, making cryptographic systems vulnerable to attacks.

Key reuse is a common mistake that can introduce vulnerabilities. When the same encryption key is used for multiple purposes or sessions, it can increase the risk of data breaches. Cryptographic best practices recommend using unique keys for different contexts to limit the impact of a compromised key.

Inadequate entropy sources for key generation can lead to vulnerabilities. Entropy sources provide the randomness needed for secure key generation. If the entropy source is insufficient or biased, it can result in weak keys that are easier for attackers to guess. Ensuring a sufficient entropy pool is essential for robust key generation.

Another vulnerability is improper handling of cryptographic errors. When cryptographic operations fail or encounter errors, it's crucial to handle them securely. Revealing specific error details can provide attackers with valuable information about the cryptographic implementation, potentially aiding in attacks. Error handling should be designed to minimize information leakage.

Key escrow or key recovery mechanisms can also introduce vulnerabilities. These mechanisms involve storing a copy of cryptographic keys with a third party, typically for law enforcement or recovery purposes. While they can be important for legal reasons, they introduce the risk of unauthorized access to keys if not properly secured and audited.

A lack of secure update mechanisms for cryptographic libraries and software can also pose vulnerabilities. Cryptographic software should be regularly updated to patch known vulnerabilities and address security issues. Failing to update cryptographic components can leave systems exposed to known exploits.

In summary, understanding and addressing common cryptographic vulnerabilities is essential for maintaining the security of digital systems and data. Weak key management, algorithmic weaknesses, flawed protocols, side-channel attacks, and other vulnerabilities can lead to breaches and data compromises. Cryptographers, developers, and security professionals must stay vigilant and adopt best practices to mitigate these vulnerabilities and ensure the continued integrity and confidentiality of cryptographic systems.

In the ever-evolving landscape of cybersecurity, the task of mitigating threats and enhancing security remains a paramount concern for organizations, individuals, and governments alike. The digital realm, with its vast networks and interconnected systems, offers tremendous opportunities but also presents an array of risks that demand vigilant and proactive measures to address.

One of the fundamental principles of cybersecurity is understanding the nature of threats. Threats can take various forms, ranging from cybercriminals seeking financial gain to nation-state actors conducting espionage or launching cyberattacks with geopolitical motivations. Recognizing the diversity of threats is crucial for developing effective security strategies.

Vulnerability assessment is a key step in mitigating threats. It involves identifying weaknesses and potential entry points that could be exploited by attackers. Vulnerabilities can exist in software, hardware, network configurations, and even human behavior. Regularly scanning and assessing systems and processes for vulnerabilities is essential for preemptive action.

Patch management is another critical aspect of cybersecurity. Many vulnerabilities arise from unpatched or outdated software. Software vendors release security patches to address known vulnerabilities, and organizations must promptly apply these patches to reduce the risk of exploitation. Delayed patching can leave systems exposed to attacks.

Security awareness and training play a vital role in enhancing security. Human error, such as falling for phishing scams or using weak passwords, remains a significant contributor to security breaches. Educating employees and users about cybersecurity best practices, threats, and safe online behavior can significantly reduce the human factor in security incidents.

Access control is fundamental to security. Restricting access to systems and data to authorized users only is a fundamental principle of cybersecurity. Employing robust access control mechanisms, such as role-based access control (RBAC) and least privilege principles, ensures that individuals have access only to the resources necessary for their roles.

Encryption is a powerful tool for enhancing data security. By encrypting data both in transit and at rest, organizations can safeguard sensitive information even if it falls into the wrong hands. Strong encryption algorithms and key management practices are essential components of effective data protection.

Multi-factor authentication (MFA) is becoming increasingly important for securing accounts and systems. MFA requires users to provide multiple forms of authentication, such as a password and a biometric scan or a one-time code sent to their mobile device. This extra layer of security makes it significantly more challenging for unauthorized individuals to gain access.

Intrusion detection and prevention systems (IDS/IPS) are critical for identifying and responding to suspicious activities and potential threats. These systems monitor network traffic and system behavior, alerting security teams to anomalies or known attack patterns. In some cases, they can also take automated actions to block malicious traffic.

Regular security audits and penetration testing provide organizations with insights into their security posture. Security experts simulate attacks to identify vulnerabilities and weaknesses. Conducting these assessments allows organizations to proactively address issues before they can be exploited by real attackers.

Incident response plans are essential for effectively handling security incidents when they occur. These plans outline the steps to take when a security breach is detected, including containment, investigation, communication, and recovery efforts. Well-prepared incident response teams can minimize the impact of security incidents.

Collaboration and information sharing within the cybersecurity community are essential. Threat intelligence sharing enables organizations to stay informed about emerging threats and attack techniques. By sharing information about threats and vulnerabilities, the community can collectively work to enhance security defenses.

Cloud security is a growing concern as organizations increasingly adopt cloud services and infrastructure. Ensuring that cloud providers have robust security measures in place is crucial. Additionally, organizations must understand their responsibilities for securing data and applications in the cloud and implement appropriate security controls.

Security by design is a principle that emphasizes building security into systems and applications from the outset. Rather than adding security as an afterthought, organizations should consider security at every stage of development and deployment. Secure coding practices and security testing are essential elements of this approach.

Threat modeling is a proactive approach to identifying and mitigating potential threats. It involves systematically analyzing a system's components, data flows, and potential attack vectors to understand where vulnerabilities may exist. By identifying threats early in the design phase, organizations can make informed decisions about security controls.

Cybersecurity standards and frameworks provide organizations with guidance for establishing robust security practices. Frameworks like NIST Cybersecurity Framework and ISO 27001 offer comprehensive approaches to managing cybersecurity risks. Adhering to recognized standards can help organizations enhance their security posture.

Continuous monitoring is essential for maintaining security over time. Threats and vulnerabilities evolve, requiring ongoing assessment and adjustment of security measures. Continuous monitoring systems provide real-time visibility into network and system behavior, enabling rapid response to emerging threats.

Cybersecurity is not a one-time effort but an ongoing commitment to adapt to the ever-changing threat landscape. Organizations must invest in security measures, train their personnel, and stay informed about the latest threats and best practices. In doing so, they can mitigate threats and enhance their security posture in an increasingly digital world.

In summary, mitigating threats and enhancing security in today's digital landscape is a multifaceted endeavor. It involves understanding the nature of threats, assessing vulnerabilities, implementing security measures, and continuously monitoring and adapting to evolving threats. Security is not a destination but a journey, and it requires the collective effort of individuals, organizations, and the cybersecurity community to stay ahead of the challenges posed by malicious actors in the digital realm.

Chapter 9: Cryptography in the Digital Age

In today's digital age, where data flows freely across networks and devices, cryptography plays a pivotal role in safeguarding data privacy and protection. The term "cryptography" itself evokes an image of secrecy and codes, but its significance goes far beyond mere secrecy—it encompasses the broader aspects of data integrity, authenticity, and confidentiality.

At its core, cryptography is the science and art of secure communication. It provides the means to transform information in such a way that it can be shared or stored securely, even in the presence of adversaries who might attempt to intercept or tamper with the data. In essence, cryptography is the guardian of digital secrets.

One of the primary functions of cryptography is ensuring the confidentiality of data. When sensitive information, such as personal messages, financial transactions, or medical records, is transmitted or stored, there's a need to keep it confidential. Cryptographic algorithms achieve this by encrypting the data, converting it into an unreadable form that can only be deciphered by those who possess the appropriate decryption key.

Consider the simple act of sending an email. When you hit the "send" button, your message traverses various networks and servers before reaching its destination. Without encryption, this message would be like an open postcard, visible to anyone who cares to look. Cryptography, in the form of email encryption protocols like Pretty Good Privacy (PGP) or Transport Layer Security

(TLS), ensures that your email content remains confidential during its journey.

Confidentiality is not the only aspect of data protection. Data integrity is equally critical. Cryptographic hashing algorithms are used to create unique fixed-length representations, or hash values, of data. These hash values serve as digital fingerprints of the original data. If the data is altered in any way, even a small change, the hash value will change dramatically, alerting users to potential tampering.

Imagine the importance of data integrity in a digital voting system. If the vote tallies were not protected against tampering, malicious actors could alter the results, undermining the trust in the electoral process. Cryptographic hashing ensures that the vote data remains intact and unaltered.

Authentication is another essential aspect of data protection. Cryptographic techniques, such as digital signatures, enable individuals and entities to prove their identity and the authenticity of the data they send. Digital signatures are created by applying a cryptographic algorithm to a message using a private key. Anyone with access to the corresponding public key can verify the signature, confirming both the sender's identity and the integrity of the message.

Consider online banking transactions, where you want assurance that the financial instructions you receive are indeed from your bank and not from a malicious actor. Cryptographic digital signatures provide that assurance by allowing the bank to sign its messages to you, making it virtually impossible for others to impersonate the bank.

As data continues to move to the cloud and across distributed systems, the need for secure key management becomes evident. Cryptographic keys are the linchpin of encryption and decryption processes. Protecting keys from unauthorized access is paramount. Cryptographic solutions, such as Hardware Security Modules (HSMs), provide a secure environment for generating, storing, and managing keys, safeguarding them against theft or misuse.

In scenarios like securing medical records in the cloud, healthcare providers rely on cryptographic key management to ensure that only authorized personnel can access sensitive patient information. Without proper key protection, the privacy of patients would be at risk.

Cryptography also plays a vital role in protecting data at rest. When data is stored on devices or servers, it may be susceptible to physical theft or unauthorized access. Full-disk encryption, as exemplified by BitLocker on Windows and FileVault on macOS, ensures that data remains encrypted when not actively in use, adding a layer of protection against unauthorized access.

Consider the use of cryptography in safeguarding the data on your smartphone. If your device were lost or stolen, the encryption of the data stored on it would make it exceedingly difficult for anyone without the correct credentials to access your personal information.

In the realm of secure communication, end-to-end encryption is a key concept. It ensures that only the sender and the intended recipient of a message can decipher its contents. Even service providers facilitating the communication cannot access the message in its decrypted form. Applications like Signal and WhatsApp use end-to-end encryption, making them highly secure options for messaging.

When discussing the role of cryptography in data privacy and protection, it's crucial to mention the delicate balance between privacy and lawful access. In some cases, law enforcement agencies may require access to encrypted data for legitimate investigative purposes. This debate over the "encryption backdoor" is a complex one, as it involves reconciling individual privacy rights with national security concerns.

Ultimately, the role of cryptography in data privacy and protection is central to our increasingly digital lives. Whether it's securing financial transactions, protecting medical records, or ensuring the confidentiality of personal communications, cryptography stands as the guardian of our digital secrets. Its continued evolution and adaptation to emerging threats are essential in an era where data is both a valuable asset and a potential target for malicious actors.

In our increasingly connected world, where data flows across borders and devices at an unprecedented rate, cryptographic innovations are at the forefront of ensuring security and privacy. As technology continues to advance, new challenges and opportunities emerge, driving the evolution of cryptography to address the demands of our interconnected digital landscape.

One of the most notable innovations in recent years is the advent of post-quantum cryptography. With the growing realization that quantum computers could pose a significant threat to existing cryptographic algorithms, researchers have been working tirelessly to develop quantum-resistant encryption methods. These new cryptographic schemes are designed to withstand the computational power of quantum computers, which could potentially break traditional encryption algorithms.

Post-quantum cryptography explores alternative mathematical approaches that are believed to be secure even in the face of quantum computing. Lattice-based cryptography, code-based cryptography, and multivariate polynomial cryptography are among the promising approaches in this field. These innovations are crucial for ensuring the long-term security of digital communications and data protection in a quantum-enabled future.

Homomorphic encryption is another groundbreaking cryptographic innovation that has far-reaching implications. It allows computations to be performed on encrypted data without the need to decrypt it. This capability opens up possibilities for secure outsourcing of computations to the cloud while keeping sensitive data confidential. Industries such as healthcare, finance, and research can benefit from this technology by harnessing the power of the cloud while maintaining data privacy.

Blockchain technology, initially developed for cryptocurrencies like Bitcoin, has evolved into a cryptographic innovation with a wide range of applications. Blockchains are decentralized, tamper-resistant ledgers that rely on cryptographic techniques for data integrity and consensus. They have found applications in supply chain management, voting systems, identity verification, and more. The immutability of blockchain data makes it a powerful tool for ensuring the integrity of records and transactions.

Zero-knowledge proofs represent a fascinating cryptographic innovation that allows one party to prove the knowledge of a specific piece of information to another party without revealing the information itself. This concept has profound implications for privacy and authentication. For example, it can enable secure authentication without sharing sensitive credentials, making it valuable for enhancing security in various online interactions. Secure multi-party computation (MPC) is an innovation that enables multiple parties to jointly compute a function over their inputs while keeping those inputs private. This cryptographic technique has applications in collaborative data analysis, privacy-preserving machine learning, and more. It allows organizations to collaborate and gain insights from data without revealing sensitive information to each other.

Quantum key distribution (QKD) is a cryptographic innovation designed to address the quantum threat by leveraging the principles of quantum mechanics. QKD enables two parties to generate a shared encryption key while detecting any eavesdropping attempts. It offers a fundamentally secure way to establish cryptographic keys and is particularly relevant for securing communications in a post-quantum world.

The field of cryptographic innovations also extends to biometric cryptosystems, where biometric data such as fingerprints, facial features, or iris patterns are used for authentication and encryption. Biometrics provide a unique and personalized approach to security, making it difficult for unauthorized individuals to gain access. Biometric cryptosystems are increasingly being adopted for secure access control and identity verification.

In the context of the Internet of Things (IoT), lightweight cryptography has emerged as a crucial innovation. IoT devices often have limited computational resources, making traditional cryptographic algorithms impractical. Lightweight cryptography focuses on designing efficient and resource-friendly encryption methods tailored for IoT environments. These innovations enable secure communication and data protection in the IoT ecosystem.

As the world becomes more interconnected, cryptographic innovations continue to evolve to meet the diverse needs of different industries and applications. Whether it's protecting sensitive data from quantum threats, enabling secure computations on encrypted data, or preserving privacy in a digital world, cryptography remains at the forefront of technological advancements.

Moreover, the ongoing collaboration between researchers, industry experts, and cryptographic communities drives the development and adoption of these innovations. Open-source cryptographic libraries and standards play a crucial role in ensuring the accessibility and interoperability of cryptographic solutions.

In summary, cryptographic innovations are instrumental in addressing the complex challenges of our connected world. From post-quantum cryptography to homomorphic encryption, blockchain technology, zero-knowledge proofs, and more, these innovations empower individuals and organizations to protect their data, secure their communications, and navigate the digital landscape with confidence. As technology continues to advance, the role of cryptography in safeguarding our digital future remains indispensable.

Chapter 10: Future Trends in Cryptography

In the realm of technology and cryptography, the emergence of quantum computing represents a paradigm shift with profound implications for the field of cybersecurity. Quantum computing, a field that harnesses the principles of quantum mechanics, promises to revolutionize computing power in ways that challenge the very foundations of modern cryptography.

At the heart of quantum computing's potential lies its ability to perform certain types of calculations at exponentially faster rates than classical computers. Classical computers use bits as the fundamental unit of information, which can represent either a 0 or a 1. Quantum computers, on the other hand, use quantum bits or qubits, which can exist in multiple states simultaneously due to the phenomenon known as superposition.

Superposition enables quantum computers to process vast amounts of information simultaneously, making them exceptionally powerful for specific tasks. One of these tasks is Shor's algorithm, a quantum algorithm developed by Peter Shor in 1994. Shor's algorithm has the potential to efficiently factor large numbers, a problem that forms the basis of widely-used encryption methods like RSA.

The ability to factor large numbers quickly has profound implications for cryptography. Many cryptographic protocols, including RSA, rely on the computational difficulty of factoring large semiprime numbers. Quantum computers, if they reach a sufficient level of maturity and scale, could potentially break these encryption schemes in a fraction of the time it would take classical computers.

This impending threat to classical encryption has prompted the need for post-quantum cryptography. Post-quantum cryptography aims to develop encryption methods that are resistant to attacks by quantum computers. These methods explore alternative mathematical problems, such as lattice-based cryptography, code-based cryptography, and multivariate polynomial cryptography, which are believed to be computationally hard for quantum computers.

Lattice-based cryptography, for example, relies on the mathematical structures known as lattices to create encryption schemes that are believed to withstand quantum attacks. Researchers are diligently working on standardizing these post-quantum cryptographic methods to ensure that organizations and individuals can transition to quantum-resistant encryption when necessary.

While quantum computing poses a significant challenge to classical encryption, it also offers potential benefits for cryptography through the development of quantum-resistant algorithms. Quantum-resistant algorithms are designed to remain secure even in the presence of quantum computers. These algorithms aim to maintain the confidentiality and integrity of data in a quantum-enabled world.

Quantum key distribution (QKD) is another area where quantum computing has a positive impact on cryptography. QKD leverages the principles of quantum mechanics to establish secure communication channels by detecting any attempts at eavesdropping. Unlike classical key distribution methods, QKD provides a fundamentally secure way to exchange cryptographic keys.

Quantum key distribution is particularly relevant for applications where the highest level of security is essential, such as secure government communications and financial transactions. The ability to detect eavesdropping attempts makes QKD a powerful tool for protecting sensitive information.

Furthermore, quantum-resistant cryptography is not the only solution to the quantum threat. Post-quantum cryptographic methods may provide security, but they often come with increased computational requirements. Quantum computers, with their exponential processing power, could potentially outperform classical computers in breaking these post-quantum schemes as well.

To mitigate this risk, researchers are exploring the use of quantum-resistant cryptographic protocols in combination with quantum key distribution. This hybrid approach combines the strengths of both quantum-resistant encryption and secure key distribution, providing a comprehensive security solution in a quantum world.

The timeline for quantum computing's impact on cryptography remains uncertain. While significant progress has been made in the development of quantum hardware and algorithms, building practical, large-scale quantum computers still faces substantial technical challenges. Quantum error correction, stability, and scalability are among the critical hurdles that must be overcome.

As quantum computing technology continues to advance, it is imperative for organizations and governments to proactively prepare for the quantum era. This preparation includes evaluating the security of current cryptographic systems, identifying sensitive data that may be at risk, and developing migration strategies to quantum-resistant encryption methods. Furthermore, collaboration between the research community, industry, and government entities is essential in addressing the quantum computing challenge. Standardization efforts and the development of quantum-safe cryptographic libraries are crucial to ensuring that quantum-resistant encryption methods are readily available and interoperable. In summary, quantum computing represents a transformative force in the field of cryptography. While it poses a significant threat to classical encryption methods, it also offers opportunities for quantum-resistant cryptography and quantum key distribution. The evolution of cryptography in response to the quantum threat is a testament to the resilience and adaptability of the field in the face of technological advancements. As quantum computing matures, the importance of secure and quantum-resistant cryptographic methods becomes increasingly evident in safeguarding the confidentiality and integrity of our digital world. In the rapidly evolving landscape of cryptography, the advent of quantum computing has ushered in a new era of challenges and opportunities. Quantum computing's computational power, derived from the principles of quantum mechanics, poses a significant threat to the security of classical cryptographic algorithms. The traditional cryptographic schemes that form the backbone of secure digital communication, such as RSA and ECC, rely on the difficulty of solving mathematical problems believed to be hard for classical computers. These problems include integer factorization and the discrete logarithm problem, which underpin the security of many encryption methods.

Quantum computers, with their ability to perform certain types of calculations exponentially faster than classical computers, threaten to undermine the security of these encryption methods. In particular, Shor's algorithm, a quantum algorithm developed by Peter Shor, has the potential to factor large numbers and compute discrete logarithms efficiently, rendering existing cryptographic systems vulnerable to attacks.

As the prospect of large-scale, practical quantum computers becomes increasingly likely, the need for post-quantum cryptography (PQC) arises. Post-quantum cryptography aims to develop encryption methods and cryptographic primitives that can resist attacks by quantum computers. It explores alternative mathematical problems that are believed to be secure even in the quantum era. One promising approach in post-quantum cryptography is lattice-based cryptography. Lattices are geometric structures with well-defined mathematical properties that form the basis for creating secure encryption schemes. Lattice-based cryptography offers a high level of security while being resistant to quantum attacks. This makes it a prime candidate for securing digital communication in the post-quantum world.

Code-based cryptography is another area of focus in PQC. It relies on the hardness of decoding linear codes, making it a strong contender for quantum-resistant encryption. The McEliece cryptosystem, an example of code-based cryptography, is designed to withstand attacks by both classical and quantum computers, making it a robust choice for securing sensitive data.

Multivariate polynomial cryptography is yet another post-quantum paradigm that explores cryptographic schemes based on solving multivariate polynomial equations. These equations are believed to be difficult for quantum computers to solve efficiently, making multivariate polynomial cryptography a promising candidate for quantum-resistant encryption.

Hash-based cryptography represents another approach to post-quantum security. It relies on the security of cryptographic hash functions, which are believed to be resistant to quantum attacks. The Merkle-Damgård construction, commonly used in hash-based cryptographic schemes, ensures data integrity and authentication even in the presence of quantum computing.

In the quest for post-quantum security, researchers and cryptographers are diligently working to standardize these new cryptographic methods. Standardization efforts are essential to ensure that secure and interoperable post-quantum cryptographic algorithms are available for widespread adoption.

Additionally, quantum key distribution (QKD) plays a vital role in post-quantum security. QKD leverages the principles of quantum mechanics to enable secure key exchange between two parties. Unlike classical key distribution methods, QKD provides a fundamentally secure way to generate cryptographic keys, as it is immune to attacks by quantum computers.

The implementation of quantum-resistant cryptography and the adoption of QKD are not the only responses to the quantum threat. Researchers are exploring the use of hybrid encryption schemes that combine classical and post-quantum cryptographic methods. This hybrid approach provides an extra layer of security by leveraging the strengths of both classical and quantum-resistant encryption.

The timeline for the arrival of practical, large-scale quantum computers remains uncertain. However, it is essential for organizations and governments to prepare for the quantum era proactively. This preparation includes evaluating the security of existing cryptographic systems, identifying data that may be at risk, and developing strategies for transitioning to quantum-resistant encryption.

Furthermore, the collaboration between the research community, industry, and governmental entities is critical in addressing the quantum challenge. Open-source post-quantum cryptographic libraries, cryptographic competitions, and research initiatives are essential components of this collaborative effort.

In summary, the advent of quantum computing has ushered in a new era of cryptography, where the security of classical cryptographic systems is being reevaluated. Post-quantum cryptography, with its focus on alternative mathematical problems and quantum-resistant encryption methods, holds the promise of securing digital communication in a quantum-enabled world.

While the timeline for practical quantum computers remains uncertain, the importance of preparing for the quantum era cannot be overstated. The ongoing collaboration between stakeholders, the development of standardized post-quantum cryptographic algorithms, and the adoption of quantum key distribution are all critical steps toward ensuring the security and resilience of our digital future.

BOOK 2
CRYPTOGRAPHIC ALGORITHMS AND PROTOCOLS
A COMPREHENSIVE GUIDE

ROB BOTWRIGHT

Chapter 1: Foundations of Cryptographic Algorithms

In the fascinating realm of cryptography, mathematical fundamentals form the very bedrock upon which the security of digital communication and information protection relies. At its core, cryptography is a mathematical science and art, driven by the elegant and complex mathematics that underpin the design and analysis of cryptographic algorithms.

One of the fundamental mathematical concepts in cryptography is the notion of encryption, which serves as the cornerstone of data security. Encryption involves the transformation of plaintext—human-readable data—into ciphertext—unreadable data that appears as random gibberish—using a mathematical algorithm and an encryption key. The security of encryption lies in the mathematical operations applied to the data and the secrecy of the encryption key.

The mathematics behind encryption is multifaceted, with various encryption algorithms employing different mathematical techniques. One widely used encryption technique is the substitution-permutation network, which rearranges and substitutes data elements in a way that is computationally secure. The Advanced Encryption Standard (AES), a symmetric key encryption algorithm, relies on these principles to protect sensitive data.

Another essential cryptographic concept is the concept of keys, both symmetric and asymmetric. Symmetric encryption algorithms use a single secret key for both encryption and decryption, making the security of the key paramount. The mathematics of symmetric key cryptography includes operations such as bitwise XOR (exclusive OR), substitution, and permutation, all executed with precision to ensure confidentiality.

On the other hand, asymmetric encryption, also known as public-key cryptography, introduces a pair of mathematically related keys: a public key and a private key. The mathematics behind asymmetric encryption leverages the computational infeasibility of deriving the private key from the public key, forming the foundation of secure digital communication. The RSA encryption algorithm, for instance, relies on the mathematical properties of prime numbers for its security.

Prime numbers themselves are a mathematical treasure trove in cryptography. The fundamental theorem of arithmetic states that every positive integer can be factored into prime numbers uniquely. This property forms the basis for cryptographic systems that rely on the difficulty of factoring large semiprime numbers, such as RSA encryption. The mathematical beauty of prime numbers becomes a formidable barrier against adversaries seeking to break encryption.

Modular arithmetic is another mathematical concept that plays a crucial role in cryptography. Modular arithmetic operates within a fixed range, or modulus, and involves operations like addition, subtraction, multiplication, and exponentiation. Cryptographic algorithms use modular arithmetic to ensure that mathematical operations wrap around within the modulus, which introduces an additional layer of complexity and security.

The concept of mathematical hardness is intrinsic to cryptography. A problem is considered "hard" if it is computationally infeasible to solve within a reasonable amount of time using available computational resources. Cryptographic algorithms are designed to rely on hard mathematical problems, such as the discrete logarithm problem or the difficulty of factoring large numbers, to ensure the security of encrypted data.

Furthermore, cryptographic hash functions are indispensable mathematical constructs in ensuring data integrity and authentication. Hash functions take an input data set and produce a fixed-length output, known as a hash value or hash code. The mathematical properties of hash functions, including collision resistance and preimage resistance, are meticulously crafted to withstand cryptographic attacks.

The notion of entropy, borrowed from information theory and probability theory, plays a pivotal role in cryptographic key generation. Entropy measures the uncertainty or randomness of data. Cryptographic systems require a high degree of entropy when generating cryptographic keys to ensure that keys are truly unpredictable and resistant to brute-force attacks.

Elliptic curve cryptography (ECC) represents yet another mathematical frontier in cryptography. ECC leverages the mathematics of elliptic curves to provide strong security with relatively small key sizes compared to traditional cryptographic systems. This mathematical elegance has made ECC a popular choice for securing modern digital communication.

In the realm of digital signatures, which authenticate the origin and integrity of digital messages, mathematical concepts like modular exponentiation and discrete logarithms come into play. Digital signatures use mathematical algorithms to generate a unique signature for a message, allowing recipients to verify the authenticity of the sender and the integrity of the message.

Quantum cryptography, a burgeoning field, introduces quantum-mechanical phenomena to enhance the security of cryptographic systems. Quantum key distribution (QKD), for instance, relies on the principles of quantum mechanics, such as superposition and entanglement, to generate and distribute secure cryptographic keys. The mathematical formalism of quantum mechanics is intertwined with the cryptographic protocols in this cutting-edge field.

In summary, the mathematical fundamentals of cryptography weave a tapestry of elegance and complexity that underlie the security of our digital world. From encryption algorithms to prime numbers, modular arithmetic to cryptographic hash functions, the mathematics of cryptography provides the tools and principles needed to protect sensitive information, ensure data integrity, and authenticate digital interactions. As technology advances, the mathematics of cryptography continues to evolve, adapting to emerging challenges and fortifying the security of our interconnected digital realm.

In the intricate world of cryptography, where the security of digital communication and data protection is paramount, the design of cryptographic algorithms rests on a foundation of meticulously crafted principles. These algorithm design principles are the guiding stars that ensure the resilience and effectiveness of cryptographic systems, enabling them to withstand the relentless scrutiny of potential adversaries.

At the core of cryptographic algorithm design lies the principle of security through obscurity. This principle, which has been debunked over time, emphasizes the idea that the secrecy of the algorithm itself should provide security. However, modern cryptographic practice adheres to the diametrically opposed concept of security through transparency. In other words, the security of a cryptographic algorithm should not rely on keeping the algorithm itself secret but rather on the strength of mathematical principles and keys.

Mathematical rigor is an essential pillar of cryptographic algorithm design. Cryptographic algorithms are grounded in mathematical concepts and properties that are rigorously analyzed and proven to withstand attacks. Rigorous mathematical analysis ensures that the security claims of an algorithm are not based on assumptions but are backed by mathematical proof.

The concept of provable security, rooted in mathematical rigor, involves demonstrating that a cryptographic algorithm is secure under specific mathematical assumptions. Provable security provides a robust framework for evaluating the strength of cryptographic algorithms by formally establishing the relationship between security properties and mathematical foundations.

Key management is a foundational principle in cryptographic algorithm design. The security of cryptographic systems hinges on the secure generation, distribution, and storage of cryptographic keys. Proper key management practices ensure that keys remain confidential and are resistant to theft or compromise.

Cryptographic algorithms are often classified into two broad categories: symmetric-key cryptography and asymmetric-key cryptography. Symmetric-key cryptography, also known as secret-key cryptography, relies on a single secret key for both encryption and decryption. The principle of symmetric-key cryptography is that the same key is used for both operations, with the security derived from the secrecy of the key itself.

The principle of key agility, an important aspect of symmetric-key cryptography, emphasizes the periodic change of encryption keys to mitigate risks associated with key compromise. Key agility ensures that even if an attacker gains access to an old key, they cannot decrypt past communications or future communications encrypted with different keys.

Asymmetric-key cryptography, also known as public-key cryptography, introduces the concept of key pairs—a public key and a private key. The mathematical relationship between the public key and private key enables secure encryption and decryption, authentication, and digital signatures. The principle of asymmetric-key cryptography is that the public key can be widely distributed while the private key remains secret.

Key exchange protocols, another fundamental aspect of cryptographic algorithm design, facilitate the secure exchange of cryptographic keys between parties. Protocols like the Diffie-Hellman key exchange rely on mathematical principles to ensure that two parties can agree on a shared secret key without revealing it to eavesdroppers.

In cryptographic algorithm design, simplicity is a guiding principle. Simplicity in cryptographic algorithms makes them easier to analyze for security properties, reduces the likelihood of implementation errors, and enhances their overall robustness. Simplicity ensures that cryptographic algorithms can be understood and implemented correctly.

Cryptographic algorithms should be resistant to known attacks, including brute-force attacks, statistical attacks, and chosen-plaintext attacks. The principle of resistance to known attacks requires that cryptographic algorithms are designed to withstand a wide range of attack scenarios and maintain the confidentiality and integrity of data.

The principle of forward secrecy, a key consideration in cryptographic protocol design, ensures that the compromise of long-term encryption keys does not jeopardize the confidentiality of past communications. Forward secrecy is achieved by using ephemeral keys for each session, which are discarded after use.

In cryptographic algorithm design, the principle of adaptability is crucial to ensure that algorithms can evolve and adapt to emerging threats. Cryptographers constantly monitor the security landscape, identify vulnerabilities, and develop updates or replacements for cryptographic algorithms as needed.

Cryptographic agility is another important principle that emphasizes the ability to switch to stronger cryptographic algorithms or key lengths in response to evolving threats. Cryptographic agility ensures that cryptographic systems can adapt to changes in the threat landscape without requiring a complete overhaul.

The principle of randomness is integral to cryptographic algorithm design. Cryptographically secure random number generation is essential for generating cryptographic keys and ensuring the unpredictability of encryption. Randomness forms the foundation of cryptographic strength and resistance to statistical attacks.

In summary, cryptographic algorithm design principles are the guiding principles that underpin the security of digital communication and data protection. These principles, rooted in mathematical rigor, transparency, and security through sound mathematical foundations, ensure that cryptographic algorithms withstand the test of time and evolving threats. Key management, simplicity, adaptability, and resistance to known attacks are essential considerations in the design of cryptographic systems that safeguard the confidentiality and integrity of our digital world.

Chapter 2: Classical Cryptographic Protocols

Delving into the intriguing history of cryptography, we embark on a journey that traces the evolution of classical cryptographic protocols, unveiling the ingenious techniques and historical contexts that shaped the field. Our exploration begins with the earliest recorded instances of cryptography, dating back to ancient civilizations, where the imperative of secrecy gave birth to rudimentary cryptographic methods.

One of the earliest known cryptographic techniques is the Caesar cipher, attributed to Julius Caesar in the first century BCE. This simple substitution cipher involved shifting each letter in the plaintext by a fixed number of positions down the alphabet, creating a ciphertext that was intelligible only to those who knew the key. The Caesar cipher served as an early example of the concept of encryption, where the transformation of data ensured its confidentiality.

Moving forward in time, we encounter the intriguing story of the Scytale, an ancient cryptographic device employed by the Spartans in 5th-century BCE Greece. The Scytale consisted of a rod and a strip of parchment, with the message written lengthwise along the rod. When unwound from the rod, the ciphertext appeared as random letters, requiring the recipient to possess a Scytale of the same dimensions to decipher the message. This early form of transposition cipher exemplified the use of physical devices to achieve cryptographic security.

The Middle Ages witnessed the development of cryptographic techniques that played pivotal roles in both military and diplomatic affairs. The Vigenère cipher, invented by Blaise de Vigenère in the 16th century, represented a significant advancement in classical cryptography. This polyalphabetic substitution cipher utilized a keyword to determine the shifting of letters in the plaintext, adding a layer of complexity compared to earlier ciphers. The Vigenère cipher perplexed codebreakers for centuries and contributed to the art of cryptographic innovation.

One of the most iconic figures in the history of classical cryptography is Auguste and Louis Lumière, creators of the Playfair cipher in the 19th century. The Playfair cipher was a digraph substitution cipher that replaced pairs of letters in the plaintext with corresponding pairs of letters in the ciphertext, based on a keyword. This technique introduced a level of security that surpassed earlier ciphers, marking a significant leap in cryptographic sophistication.

The 20th century ushered in a new era of classical cryptography with the invention of the Enigma machine, a mechanical rotor-based cipher device employed by the German military during World War II. The Enigma machine generated complex ciphertext through a series of rotors and electrical connections, making it exceptionally challenging to decrypt. The successful cryptanalysis of the Enigma code by Allied codebreakers, including Alan Turing and his team at Bletchley Park, marked a historic achievement in the annals of cryptography.

Simultaneously, the development of classical cryptographic protocols extended beyond military applications into the realm of secure communication. The one-time pad, a provably secure encryption method based on the use of a perfectly random key that is as long as the plaintext, emerged as a cornerstone of information security. Its mathematical foundation in information theory rendered it unbreakable, provided that the key remained truly random and was never reused.

In the post-World War II era, the advent of computers ushered in a new era of cryptographic research and innovation. Pioneering work by cryptographers like Claude Shannon led to the formalization of cryptographic principles, including the concept of perfect secrecy. The Diffie-Hellman key exchange, introduced in the 1970s, revolutionized secure key exchange by allowing two parties to agree on a secret key over an insecure channel.

The Data Encryption Standard (DES), adopted by the U.S. government in the 1970s, marked a significant milestone in cryptographic history as the first widely adopted encryption standard. DES utilized a Feistel network structure, which involved repeated rounds of substitution and permutation, to encrypt data. Although DES ultimately proved vulnerable to brute-force attacks due to its small key size, it paved the way for subsequent encryption standards and cryptographic protocols.

The 1990s witnessed the emergence of the Advanced Encryption Standard (AES), a symmetric-key encryption algorithm selected through an open competition organized by the U.S. National Institute of Standards and Technology (NIST). AES, based on the Rijndael algorithm, offered a higher level of security with larger key sizes and became the de facto standard for symmetric-key encryption worldwide.

The development of public-key cryptography, a groundbreaking innovation in the 1970s, fundamentally changed the landscape of cryptographic protocols. The RSA algorithm, developed by Ron Rivest, Adi Shamir, and Leonard Adleman, introduced the concept of asymmetric encryption, where a pair of keys—one public and one private—enabled secure communication without the need for a shared secret key.

Public-key infrastructure (PKI) protocols, such as X.509, provided a framework for managing digital certificates and authentication in the digital age. Digital signatures, another essential component of public-key cryptography, allowed individuals and organizations to verify the authenticity and integrity of digital messages.

The Internet era brought forth cryptographic protocols that underpin secure online communication. The Secure Sockets Layer (SSL) and its successor, Transport Layer Security (TLS), introduced encryption and authentication mechanisms for web browsers and servers, ensuring the privacy and security of online transactions and communications.

In the modern era, cryptographic protocols continue to evolve in response to emerging technologies and threats. Quantum-resistant cryptography, blockchain-based protocols, and post-quantum cryptography represent the forefront of cryptographic research, addressing the challenges posed by quantum computing and the evolving digital landscape.

In summary, the historical development of classical cryptographic protocols is a captivating journey that spans millennia, from the rudimentary ciphers of ancient civilizations to the sophisticated algorithms and protocols of the digital age. The evolution of cryptography reflects the relentless pursuit of security and privacy in an ever-changing world, where cryptographic innovation remains at the forefront of safeguarding our digital interactions and information.

As we delve deeper into the world of classical cryptographic protocols, it becomes essential to examine their strengths and weaknesses, understanding the trade-offs and considerations that shape their adoption and implementation. Classical protocols, born of historical innovation and mathematical principles, have long served as the foundation of secure communication and data protection.

One of the notable strengths of classical cryptographic protocols lies in their historical resilience. Protocols like the Caesar cipher, despite their simplicity, have demonstrated the ability to protect sensitive information in various contexts throughout history. This resilience stems from the fundamental mathematical principles that underpin classical cryptography, providing a level of security that can withstand many types of attacks.

Additionally, classical cryptographic protocols are often characterized by their efficiency and speed. Algorithms like the Vigenère cipher and the Playfair cipher, while offering a higher level of security than earlier methods, remain relatively quick to compute, making them suitable for practical use in various applications.

Moreover, classical cryptographic protocols are often easy to implement, even with limited computational resources. This accessibility has historically made them accessible to a wide range of users, from individuals seeking to protect personal communications to military and diplomatic organizations requiring secure communication channels.

However, it is important to recognize that classical cryptographic protocols have their share of weaknesses, which have become increasingly evident in the face of modern computational power and cryptographic advancements.

One significant weakness lies in the vulnerability of classical encryption methods to brute-force attacks. Brute-force attacks involve systematically trying every possible key until the correct one is found. The effectiveness of brute-force attacks is amplified by the growing computational capabilities of modern computers, making it imperative to use longer keys and more robust encryption methods.

Another weakness of classical cryptographic protocols is their susceptibility to known-plaintext attacks. In known-plaintext attacks, an attacker possesses both the ciphertext and the corresponding plaintext for one or more messages. This information can be used to deduce the encryption key or gain insights into the encryption method, potentially compromising the security of the protocol.

Cryptanalysis, the art and science of breaking cryptographic codes, has historically exploited patterns and weaknesses in classical cryptographic protocols. The advent of powerful computers and sophisticated cryptanalysis techniques has significantly increased the speed and efficiency of attacks against classical ciphers.

Furthermore, classical cryptographic protocols often lack the concept of perfect forward secrecy. Perfect forward secrecy ensures that the compromise of long-term encryption keys does not retroactively compromise the confidentiality of past communications. Classical protocols, particularly those relying on fixed keys, do not inherently provide this level of security.

The reliance on secret keys, whether symmetric or asymmetric, introduces the challenge of key management. Safeguarding and distributing cryptographic keys securely can be a complex and error-prone process, especially when dealing with large-scale communication systems or distributed networks.

As we contemplate the strengths and weaknesses of classical cryptographic protocols, it becomes evident that they have played a pivotal role in the historical evolution of cryptography. While they continue to provide valuable insights into cryptographic principles and remain relevant in specific use cases, they must be viewed within the context of modern security requirements and threats.

In today's interconnected and digital world, where the volume and sensitivity of data have grown exponentially, classical cryptographic protocols often need to be supplemented or replaced by more robust and modern encryption methods.

Symmetric-key encryption algorithms, for instance, have evolved to include the use of larger key sizes and advanced encryption modes to enhance security and resist brute-force attacks. The adoption of the Advanced Encryption Standard (AES) is a testament to the ongoing effort to improve the strength of symmetric-key encryption.

Public-key cryptography, with its asymmetric key pairs and complex mathematical underpinnings, has addressed many of the weaknesses of classical symmetric-key cryptography. Public-key protocols like RSA and elliptic curve cryptography (ECC) have become integral components of secure digital communication, providing a higher level of security and key management flexibility.

To counter known-plaintext attacks and cryptographic vulnerabilities, cryptographic research has led to the development of modern cryptographic primitives and protocols that offer enhanced security properties. These include authenticated encryption schemes, digital signatures, and secure key exchange protocols.

Moreover, the concept of cryptographic agility has gained prominence in the design and implementation of cryptographic systems. Cryptographic agility allows organizations and protocols to adapt to emerging threats by supporting multiple encryption algorithms and key lengths, facilitating the transition to more secure cryptographic methods.

In summary, classical cryptographic protocols, with their rich history and foundational principles, have served as the building blocks of secure communication for centuries. While they possess strengths in terms of historical resilience, efficiency, and accessibility, they also exhibit weaknesses in the face of modern computational capabilities and advanced cryptanalysis techniques.

As we navigate the complex landscape of information security, it is essential to recognize that classical cryptographic protocols, while valuable, are not always sufficient to address contemporary security challenges. Modern cryptographic advancements, such as longer key lengths, robust encryption algorithms, and the integration of forward secrecy and cryptographic agility, offer a path forward in enhancing the security of digital communication and data protection.

Chapter 3: Modern Block Ciphers

As we journey deeper into the intricate realm of cryptography, we encounter the fascinating principles and operations that underlie modern block ciphers—a cornerstone of secure communication and data protection in our digital age. Block ciphers are cryptographic algorithms that operate on fixed-size blocks of data, transforming plaintext into ciphertext through a series of intricate and mathematically rigorous steps.

At the heart of modern block ciphers lies the concept of confusion and diffusion, as formulated by Claude Shannon, one of the pioneers of modern cryptography. Confusion refers to the complexity and unpredictability introduced by the encryption algorithm, while diffusion involves spreading the influence of individual plaintext bits across multiple ciphertext bits. These principles collectively contribute to the strength and security of block ciphers.

The operation of a block cipher begins with the division of the plaintext into fixed-size blocks, typically 64 or 128 bits in length. Each block undergoes a series of transformations, including substitution and permutation, to generate the ciphertext. The primary components of a block cipher are the substitution boxes (S-boxes), the permutation boxes (P-boxes), and the encryption key.

S-boxes serve as the foundation of confusion within the block cipher. These nonlinear functions replace specific bits or groups of bits in the plaintext block with values determined by the encryption key. The choice of S-boxes and their mathematical properties play a critical role in the security of the cipher, as they introduce a layer of complexity that resists cryptanalysis.

P-boxes, or permutation boxes, contribute to the diffusion aspect of the block cipher. These functions rearrange the bits of the data block according to predefined patterns, ensuring that the influence of any single plaintext bit spreads across multiple ciphertext bits. The permutation process is designed to be reversible, allowing for decryption by applying the inverse permutation.

The encryption key, a fundamental component of block ciphers, is a secret value that determines the specific transformations applied during encryption and decryption. The key size directly impacts the security of the block cipher, as a larger key space makes it computationally infeasible for attackers to perform exhaustive key searches.

One of the most renowned modern block ciphers is the Data Encryption Standard (DES), introduced in the 1970s. DES operates on 64-bit blocks of data and employs a 56-bit key for encryption. Its Feistel network structure, involving repeated rounds of substitution, permutation, and key mixing, exemplifies the principles of confusion and diffusion.

However, the limited key size of DES rendered it vulnerable to brute-force attacks, prompting the development of the Advanced Encryption Standard (AES). AES, a symmetric-key block cipher, supports key sizes of 128, 192, or 256 bits and operates on 128-bit data blocks. Its strength lies in the mathematical properties of the Rijndael algorithm, which combines substitution, permutation, and key expansion to create a highly secure encryption process.

In the operation of AES, the plaintext undergoes a series of transformations, including substitution with S-boxes, row-wise permutation, column-wise mixing, and key addition in multiple rounds. This intricate process ensures that the encryption key influences the ciphertext in a manner that resists attacks.

Modern block ciphers also implement modes of operation that dictate how the encryption and decryption processes are applied to data of varying lengths. These modes, such as Electronic Codebook (ECB), Cipher Block Chaining (CBC), and Galois/Counter Mode (GCM), offer flexibility and adaptability to different application scenarios.

The Electronic Codebook (ECB) mode, for instance, encrypts individual data blocks independently, which is suitable for scenarios where each block is distinct. However, ECB mode is susceptible to certain vulnerabilities, such as the exposure of patterns in the plaintext.

In contrast, Cipher Block Chaining (CBC) mode introduces an element of feedback, where each ciphertext block is dependent on the previous ciphertext block. This chaining property adds an extra layer of security and prevents patterns from emerging in the ciphertext. CBC mode is widely used in secure communications and data storage applications.

Galois/Counter Mode (GCM), an authenticated encryption mode, combines counter mode encryption with Galois field multiplication to provide both confidentiality and authenticity. GCM is highly efficient and is commonly used in securing network communications, including the transport layer security (TLS) protocol.

As we analyze the principles and operation of modern block ciphers, it becomes evident that their design is rooted in a delicate balance of mathematical rigor, cryptographic principles, and practical considerations. These ciphers exemplify the evolution of cryptographic techniques from the pioneering days of DES to the robust and versatile AES, all while adhering to the principles of confusion and diffusion to provide a secure foundation for our digital world.

The use of block ciphers extends far beyond data encryption; they play a crucial role in securing communications, protecting stored data, and ensuring the integrity of digital transactions. With ongoing advancements in cryptography, the principles and operation of modern block ciphers continue to evolve to meet the ever-increasing demands for security and privacy in our interconnected society.

Navigating the multifaceted world of block ciphers, we encounter an essential aspect of their application: modes of operation, which govern how these ciphers encrypt and decrypt data in various scenarios, providing flexibility and adaptability for a wide range of cryptographic tasks.

Imagine a scenario where you need to encrypt a series of data blocks that may have repeating patterns, and you desire a more secure encryption than the Electronic Codebook (ECB) mode offers. In this context, Cipher Block Chaining (CBC) mode steps in as an effective choice.

CBC mode introduces an element of feedback into the encryption process. Instead of encrypting each data block in isolation, CBC mode ensures that each ciphertext block depends on the previous ciphertext block. This chaining property mitigates the vulnerability of ECB mode to exposing patterns in the plaintext, enhancing the security of the encrypted data.

The operation of CBC mode begins with the initialization vector (IV), a unique value that serves as the starting point for the encryption process. The IV is XORed with the first plaintext block to produce the first ciphertext block. Subsequently, each ciphertext block influences the encryption of the next plaintext block, creating a chain of interdependencies.

The chaining mechanism in CBC mode ensures that identical plaintext blocks will produce different ciphertext blocks when they occur at different positions in the data stream. This property adds a layer of confusion to the encryption process, making it more resistant to cryptanalysis.

One important consideration in CBC mode is the need for a random and unpredictable IV for each encryption operation. Reusing the same IV can lead to vulnerabilities, as it would result in identical ciphertext blocks for identical plaintext blocks. To maintain security, the IV must be unique and kept secret along with the encryption key.

Cipher Feedback (CFB) mode is another mode of operation that provides a flexible solution when working with smaller data units, such as individual bytes or bits. In CFB mode, the block cipher operates as a stream cipher, generating a keystream that is XORed with the plaintext to produce the ciphertext.

The keystream generation process in CFB mode begins with an IV, similar to CBC mode. However, in CFB mode, the IV is not used to encrypt the plaintext directly. Instead, it is encrypted to produce the first keystream block, which is XORed with the first plaintext block to generate the first ciphertext block. This process continues iteratively, with each ciphertext block feeding into the generation of the next keystream block.

CFB mode offers advantages in scenarios where the length of the plaintext does not align with the block size of the cipher. Unlike ECB and CBC modes, CFB mode does not require padding, as it operates at the bit level, allowing for the encryption of individual bits or bytes.

Output Feedback (OFB) mode is yet another mode that transforms a block cipher into a stream cipher. OFB mode is characterized by its ability to transform a block cipher into a synchronous stream cipher, where the keystream is generated independently of the plaintext.

In OFB mode, the IV is encrypted to produce the initial keystream block, which is then XORed with the plaintext to generate the first ciphertext block. Subsequently, the keystream block is encrypted again to produce the next keystream block, and this process continues sequentially, producing a keystream that is independent of the plaintext.

OFB mode's independence from the plaintext allows for parallelization of encryption and decryption processes, making it suitable for scenarios where efficiency and speed are paramount.

However, OFB mode does not offer error propagation. If a bit error occurs during transmission, it affects only the corresponding bit in the decrypted plaintext, and the error does not propagate to adjacent bits. This can be advantageous in situations where error correction mechanisms are in place.

Counter (CTR) mode, also known as Integer Counter Mode, is a mode of operation that transforms a block cipher into a stream cipher, similar to OFB mode. CTR mode operates by treating the IV as a counter, incrementing it for each data block to generate a unique keystream block for that block.

The counter value is encrypted to produce the keystream block, which is then XORed with the plaintext to produce the ciphertext. For each subsequent block, the counter is incremented, generating a new keystream block. This process continues until the entire plaintext is encrypted.

CTR mode offers several advantages, including parallelization of encryption and decryption processes, as well as the absence of error propagation. It is well-suited for scenarios where speed and efficiency are critical, such as in disk encryption and secure communications.

To enhance security, it is essential to use a unique counter value for each encryption operation and ensure that the counter does not repeat. Reusing counter values can lead to vulnerabilities, as it would result in the same keystream blocks for identical plaintext blocks.

The Galois/Counter Mode (GCM) combines the Counter (CTR) mode of operation with Galois field multiplication to provide both confidentiality and authenticity. GCM is widely used in securing network communications, including the Transport Layer Security (TLS) protocol.

In GCM, the counter value is encrypted to produce the keystream block, which is then used for encryption as in CTR mode. Additionally, GCM incorporates authentication by computing a Message Authentication Code (MAC) over the ciphertext and additional data, ensuring the integrity and authenticity of the communication.

In summary, modes of operation for block ciphers are essential tools in the cryptographic toolbox, providing adaptable and secure solutions for encrypting data in various scenarios. Whether it's the chaining properties of CBC mode, the bit-level encryption of CFB mode, the independence of OFB mode, or the efficiency of CTR mode, each mode offers unique benefits to address specific encryption requirements. Understanding these modes and their characteristics is crucial for effectively securing digital communication and data protection.

Chapter 4: Stream Ciphers and Pseudorandom Generators

As we delve deeper into the fascinating world of cryptography, we encounter an equally intriguing class of encryption algorithms known as stream ciphers, which differ from block ciphers in their approach to data encryption.

Stream ciphers are designed to encrypt data on a continuous stream, such as a real-time data transmission or a continuous data feed, where each element of the plaintext is encrypted individually.

Imagine a scenario where you're encrypting a live video stream or a voice call over the internet. In such cases, you need a method to encrypt the data as it flows, without the need to wait for complete blocks of data to accumulate, as is common with block ciphers. Stream ciphers are the answer to this challenge.

The fundamental concept of stream ciphers lies in their ability to generate a pseudorandom keystream, a sequence of bits that appear random, but are generated using a predetermined algorithm and an encryption key.

This keystream is then combined with the plaintext using a simple bitwise operation, typically XOR (exclusive OR), to produce the ciphertext. The XOR operation ensures that the encryption is reversible, making decryption straightforward.

One of the key advantages of stream ciphers is their efficiency in real-time applications, as they can encrypt data as it arrives or is generated. This efficiency is particularly crucial in scenarios where low latency and high data throughput are paramount.

To achieve this efficiency, stream ciphers rely on a key stream generator, which is responsible for producing the pseudorandom keystream based on the encryption key. The keystream generator is initialized with the encryption key, and its output is used to encrypt the plaintext bit by bit or byte by byte, depending on the implementation.

The pseudorandom nature of the keystream is essential for security, as it ensures that the same plaintext will be encrypted differently each time it is encountered, even with the same key. This property prevents attackers from identifying patterns in the ciphertext, making it challenging to conduct cryptanalysis.

One well-known stream cipher is the Vernam cipher, also called the one-time pad. The Vernam cipher is theoretically unbreakable when used correctly. It relies on a keystream that is as long as the plaintext and generated using truly random values. When the keystream is XORed with the plaintext, it produces ciphertext that is statistically indistinguishable from random noise.

However, the Vernam cipher faces practical limitations due to the challenges of generating and securely distributing truly random keys of the same length as the plaintext, which is often impractical.

To address these challenges, modern stream ciphers use pseudorandom number generators (PRNGs) to generate the keystream. PRNGs are algorithms that produce sequences of numbers that appear random but are generated deterministically from an initial seed value, which is typically the encryption key.

The security of a stream cipher relies heavily on the quality of the PRNG used to generate the keystream. If the PRNG is predictable or exhibits patterns, it can become vulnerable to cryptanalysis.

One widely used stream cipher is the Rivest Cipher (RC4), which gained popularity in various cryptographic protocols, including the Wired Equivalent Privacy (WEP) protocol for wireless networks and the Transport Layer Security (TLS) protocol for secure web communication.

RC4 generates a keystream based on a secret key and an initialization vector (IV). The keystream is then used to encrypt and decrypt data on a byte-by-byte basis.

While stream ciphers offer efficiency and versatility in various applications, they are not without their challenges. One of the key considerations is the management of the initialization vector (IV), which must be unique for each encryption operation.

Reusing the same IV can lead to vulnerabilities, as it may result in repeating keystreams, allowing attackers to deduce information about the plaintext. Therefore, proper IV management is crucial in stream cipher implementations.

Another challenge is ensuring the security of the pseudorandom number generator (PRNG) used to generate the keystream. Weaknesses or predictability in the PRNG can compromise the security of the entire stream cipher.

In recent years, stream ciphers have faced scrutiny in the face of emerging cryptographic threats, such as those posed by quantum computers. Quantum computers have the potential to break certain encryption schemes, including some stream ciphers, through algorithms like Shor's algorithm.

To address these challenges, ongoing research and development in the field of stream ciphers focus on the creation of post-quantum stream ciphers that remain secure in the era of quantum computing.

In summary, stream ciphers are a vital component of modern cryptography, offering efficient and versatile solutions for encrypting data streams in real-time applications. Their ability to generate pseudorandom keystreams, combined with proper key and IV management, ensures the security and confidentiality of data in various scenarios, from wireless communications to secure web browsing. As the field of cryptography continues to evolve, stream ciphers will play a crucial role in addressing emerging threats and maintaining the security of digital communication.

As we continue our exploration of stream ciphers, we delve into a crucial component of their operation: pseudorandom number generators (PRNGs) and their role in generating the pseudorandom keystreams that secure the confidentiality of data in real-time applications.

Imagine a situation where you need to encrypt a continuous stream of data, such as a video call or a live sensor feed. In such cases, you require a source of randomness to create a keystream that appears random to anyone intercepting the encrypted data, making it extremely challenging for them to decipher the original content.

Pseudorandom number generators are the answer to this challenge. PRNGs are algorithms that generate sequences of numbers that, while not truly random, exhibit the statistical properties of randomness and are computationally indistinguishable from true random numbers.

The term "pseudorandom" distinguishes these numbers from truly random numbers, as they are generated deterministically from an initial value called a seed. However, a well-designed PRNG ensures that, given the same seed, the generated sequence appears random and unpredictable.

In the context of stream ciphers, PRNGs play a pivotal role in generating the keystream—the sequence of bits or bytes that is combined with the plaintext to produce the ciphertext. The keystream must exhibit the characteristics of randomness to ensure the security of the encryption.

PRNGs are initialized with a secret key, which provides the initial seed value. This key is crucial to the security of the encryption, as it determines the uniqueness and unpredictability of the keystream. A secure encryption key, combined with a robust PRNG, is essential for protecting data confidentiality.

One widely used PRNG in stream ciphers is the Linear Feedback Shift Register (LFSR). LFSR is a shift register whose contents are shifted one bit at a time based on a linear combination of its previous contents. The output bit of the LFSR is then used as a pseudorandom bit for the keystream.

The security of an LFSR-based PRNG relies on the choice of its feedback coefficients, which determine the linear combination applied to the register's contents. Properly chosen feedback coefficients ensure that the LFSR exhibits desirable randomness properties and resists cryptanalysis.

Another PRNG commonly used in stream ciphers is the Nonlinear Feedback Shift Register (NLFSR). Unlike the LFSR, which uses linear feedback, the NLFSR employs nonlinear feedback functions that introduce additional complexity and security into the keystream generation process.

The use of NLFSRs in PRNGs contributes to the unpredictability and statistical randomness of the generated keystream, making it more resistant to cryptanalysis. NLFSRs offer a higher degree of security compared to LFSRs but require additional computational resources.

Cryptographically secure stream ciphers rely on well-designed PRNGs that meet stringent criteria for randomness, unpredictability, and resistance to cryptanalysis. These criteria ensure that the keystream generated by the PRNG appears indistinguishable from true randomness, providing a solid foundation for encrypting real-time data streams.

However, it's important to note that the security of stream ciphers is not solely dependent on the PRNG. Proper key management, initialization vector (IV) management, and the encryption algorithm itself all play crucial roles in ensuring the security of the encrypted data.

To enhance the security of PRNG-based stream ciphers, it is essential to follow best practices in key management. This includes using strong encryption keys that are sufficiently long and random, as well as securely distributing and storing these keys.

Additionally, the management of the IV is critical. The IV should be unique for each encryption operation to prevent patterns from emerging in the keystream, which could be exploited by attackers. Proper IV management is essential to maintaining the security of the encryption.

One of the significant challenges in the field of cryptography is the ongoing threat posed by quantum computers. Quantum computers have the potential to break certain encryption schemes, including those used in stream ciphers, through algorithms like Shor's algorithm.

To address this challenge, research is ongoing to develop post-quantum cryptography, which aims to create encryption algorithms and PRNGs that remain secure in the era of quantum computing. These efforts seek to ensure the long-term security of data in a rapidly evolving technological landscape.

In summary, pseudorandom number generators are a fundamental component of stream ciphers, playing a critical role in generating the pseudorandom keystreams that protect the confidentiality of data in real-time applications. Well-designed PRNGs, combined with proper key and IV management, are essential for ensuring the security of encrypted data. As the field of cryptography continues to evolve, PRNGs will remain a central focus in the development of secure encryption techniques.

Chapter 5: Public Key Infrastructure (PKI)

In our exploration of cryptography, we come across a pivotal infrastructure that underpins the secure communication and authentication on the internet: the Public Key Infrastructure, often referred to as PKI. Understanding the architecture and components of a PKI is essential for appreciating its role in establishing trust and confidentiality in the digital realm.

Imagine a scenario where you visit a website and want to ensure that the connection is secure and the website is legitimate. PKI is the framework that allows you to trust the website's identity and encrypt the data exchanged, safeguarding it from eavesdroppers.

At the heart of a PKI lies the concept of asymmetric cryptography, which involves pairs of keys: a public key and a private key. These keys work in tandem to achieve secure communication and authentication.

The public key, as the name suggests, is openly available and can be freely distributed. It serves as a means for others to encrypt data that only the corresponding private key holder can decrypt. In contrast, the private key is kept secret and is used to decrypt data encrypted with the corresponding public key.

To establish trust and authenticity, public keys are associated with entities, such as individuals, organizations, or servers. This association is made through digital certificates, which are at the core of a PKI.

A digital certificate contains the public key of an entity, along with information about the entity, such as its name, and is signed by a trusted third party called a Certificate

Authority (CA). This signature by the CA attests to the authenticity of the public key and its association with the entity.

The Certificate Authority plays a critical role in a PKI. CAs are entities that are trusted to verify the identities of individuals, organizations, or servers and issue digital certificates accordingly. They form the foundation of trust in the digital world.

When you connect to a secure website, your browser checks the website's digital certificate, which is issued by a trusted CA. If the certificate is valid and the website's public key matches the one in the certificate, your browser trusts that the website is indeed what it claims to be.

The CA's role is to verify the identity of the website owner, ensuring that the public key in the certificate is associated with the correct entity. This verification process involves a series of checks, such as confirming the ownership of the domain and validating the organization's legal status.

In addition to the Certificate Authority, there are other essential components in a PKI ecosystem. One of these components is the Registration Authority (RA). The RA acts as an intermediary between the entity requesting a certificate (the end-user) and the CA. It verifies the identity of the entity, collects necessary information, and submits the certificate request to the CA.

Certificate Revocation Lists (CRLs) are another critical element. CRLs are lists maintained by CAs that contain information about certificates that have been revoked before their expiration date. This is crucial for promptly revoking certificates in cases of compromise or other security incidents.

To ensure the integrity and authenticity of certificates, PKI relies on cryptographic algorithms and digital signatures. Digital signatures, generated using the private key of the CA, provide assurance that the certificate has not been tampered with during transmission.

A critical aspect of a PKI is the hierarchical trust model. This model involves a hierarchy of CAs, with a root CA at the top. The root CA is the highest authority and is self-signed, meaning its certificate is signed with its private key. The root CA's public key is distributed widely and forms the foundation of trust in the entire PKI.

Beneath the root CA, there are intermediate CAs that may issue certificates on behalf of the root CA. These intermediates are trusted by the root CA and can, in turn, issue certificates for entities or subordinate CAs further down the hierarchy.

This hierarchical trust model allows for scalability and delegation of trust. Organizations can operate their subordinate CAs, which issue certificates to their employees or servers, and these certificates are trusted because they can be traced back to a trusted root CA.

A crucial part of a PKI's architecture is the certificate store or repository, where digital certificates are stored and managed. This repository can be distributed across multiple servers and locations to ensure redundancy and availability.

In summary, a Public Key Infrastructure (PKI) is the framework that enables secure communication and authentication in the digital world. At its core, PKI relies on the use of public and private keys, digital certificates issued by trusted Certificate Authorities (CAs), and a hierarchical trust model. These components work together to establish trust, verify identities, and safeguard data in a manner that is fundamental to the security of the internet and digital communications.

In our ongoing exploration of the Public Key Infrastructure (PKI), we come across an integral concept: digital certificates and the trust models that form the bedrock of security and trust in the digital realm.

Imagine you're browsing the internet, and you want to make sure that the website you're visiting is authentic and that your connection with it is secure. Digital certificates are the key to this assurance, and trust models define how this assurance is established.

Digital certificates, often referred to as public-key certificates or simply certificates, are a fundamental component of PKI. At their core, these certificates are a means of associating a public key with the identity of an individual, organization, or server in a way that can be trusted by others.

Think of a digital certificate as a digital ID card. It contains essential information such as the public key, the entity's name (like a website domain or an organization's name), a serial number, and the expiration date of the certificate. This information is bundled together and signed by a trusted third party called a Certificate Authority (CA).

The CA's signature on the certificate serves as a stamp of authenticity and trust. It confirms that the public key in the certificate indeed belongs to the entity identified in the certificate. In essence, the CA vouches for the legitimacy of the certificate holder's public key.

The concept of digital certificates is built on the principles of asymmetric cryptography, where a pair of keys—public and private—work together. The public key is shared openly and is used to encrypt data that only the corresponding private key can decrypt. In the context of digital certificates, the public key is included in the certificate, while the private key is kept securely by the certificate holder.

To establish trust in a digital certificate, it's not enough for an entity to generate its own certificate and claim authenticity. This is where Certificate Authorities come into play. CAs are entities that are trusted to verify the identities of individuals, organizations, or servers and issue digital certificates accordingly.

Imagine a CA as an impartial third party that conducts thorough background checks and verification processes before issuing a certificate. This verification may include confirming domain ownership for a website, checking an organization's legal status, or validating an individual's identity.

Once the CA is satisfied that the entity's identity is legitimate, it signs the certificate with its private key. This signature is what ties the certificate to the CA and bestows trust upon it. When you visit a website and see a padlock icon in your browser's address bar, it means that the website's digital certificate has been signed by a trusted CA, assuring you of its authenticity.

Now, let's delve into trust models within PKI. Trust models define how trust is established and managed in a PKI ecosystem. There are several trust models, but the two most common ones are the hierarchical trust model and the web of trust.

In the hierarchical trust model, trust is organized in a hierarchical structure, similar to a tree. At the top of the hierarchy is the root CA, which is self-signed and forms the ultimate authority. Beneath the root CA, there are intermediate CAs that are trusted by the root CA and can issue certificates for entities or subordinate CAs further down the hierarchy.

This hierarchical approach provides a clear chain of trust. Certificates issued by intermediate CAs are trusted because they can be traced back to the root CA. This model is often used in large organizations, where the root CA is operated by the organization itself.

On the other hand, the web of trust is a decentralized trust model commonly associated with Pretty Good Privacy (PGP) and other similar systems. In this model, individuals can vouch for the authenticity of other individuals' public keys by digitally signing them. Over time, a network of trust is built, where trust is not centralized but distributed among users.

In the web of trust, trust is based on the collective trustworthiness of individuals within the network. If you trust someone's judgment and they vouch for the authenticity of a public key, you may choose to trust that key as well. This model is often seen in email encryption and other peer-to-peer communication systems.

Both trust models have their strengths and weaknesses. The hierarchical model offers a clear structure and centralized management, making it suitable for large organizations and enterprise environments. The web of trust, on the other hand, emphasizes decentralization and user autonomy, making it flexible and adaptable for individual users.

Digital certificates and trust models play a pivotal role in securing online communications, e-commerce, and authentication. They provide the essential framework for establishing trust in a digital world where identities and authenticity must be verified reliably. As we continue our journey into the realm of cryptography and PKI, we'll explore how these concepts come together to create a secure and trustworthy digital environment.

Chapter 6: Digital Signatures and Authentication

In our exploration of cryptography and its vital role in secure digital communication, we encounter a critical concept: digital signatures and their profound importance in the realm of information security.

Imagine a world where you could digitally sign documents, contracts, or messages with the same level of authenticity and legal validity as physical signatures. Digital signatures make this a reality, offering a powerful tool for ensuring the integrity, authenticity, and non-repudiation of digital data.

At its core, a digital signature is a cryptographic mechanism that enables the verification of the origin and integrity of a message or document. It serves as the digital equivalent of a handwritten signature, but with added layers of security and efficiency.

To understand how digital signatures work, let's first explore the basic principles of asymmetric cryptography. In this cryptographic scheme, there are two related but distinct keys: a public key and a private key. The public key is openly available and can be shared with anyone, while the private key is kept secret and known only to the owner.

When a user wants to create a digital signature for a document or message, they use their private key to perform a mathematical operation on the data. This operation generates a unique string of characters, known as the digital signature, which is specific to that document and the private key used to create it.

Crucially, the digital signature is tied to the content of the document in such a way that even a minor change in the document would result in a completely different signature. This property ensures the integrity of the data; any tampering with the document would be immediately detected when verifying the signature.

The recipient of the digitally signed document or message uses the sender's public key to verify the signature. They apply a corresponding mathematical operation to the received signature and the document's content. If the resulting value matches a specific criterion, the signature is considered valid. Otherwise, it is rejected.

The magic of digital signatures lies in their ability to provide strong authentication and non-repudiation. When a sender signs a document with their private key, they are essentially saying, "I am the one who sent this, and I stand by its content." This assertion is backed by the mathematical properties of asymmetric cryptography.

In the digital world, authentication is paramount. It ensures that you are indeed communicating with the intended party and not an imposter. Digital signatures achieve this by tying the signature to the sender's private key, which only they possess. Therefore, if a document bears a valid digital signature from a particular sender, it is virtually irrefutable proof of the sender's identity.

Non-repudiation is equally vital, especially in legal and business contexts. When a sender digitally signs a contract or agreement, they cannot later deny their involvement or disown the content. The digital signature provides indisputable evidence of the sender's consent and commitment to the document.

Digital signatures are not limited to individual messages or documents; they can also be applied to software, ensuring that software updates come from legitimate sources and have not been tampered with. This safeguards users against malicious software and ensures the integrity of software distribution channels.

Furthermore, digital signatures are an integral part of the Public Key Infrastructure (PKI), where they play a role in verifying the authenticity of digital certificates issued by Certificate Authorities (CAs). When you connect to a secure website, your browser uses the website's digital certificate to establish a secure connection, and digital signatures ensure the trustworthiness of these certificates.

One of the key advantages of digital signatures is their efficiency and convenience. Unlike physical signatures that require the exchange of physical documents or face-to-face meetings, digital signatures can be applied and verified electronically, saving time and resources.

However, it's important to note that the security of digital signatures hinges on the proper safeguarding of private keys. If an attacker gains access to a user's private key, they can impersonate that user and create fraudulent digital signatures. Thus, the protection of private keys is of paramount importance.

To enhance security, hardware-based security modules (HSMs) are often employed to store and manage private keys securely. These devices provide an additional layer of protection against key theft or compromise.

In summary, digital signatures are a cornerstone of modern cryptography and information security. They enable strong authentication, integrity verification, and non-repudiation in the digital realm, ensuring the trustworthiness of digital data, documents, and communications. As we continue to navigate the intricate landscape of cryptography, digital signatures remain a crucial tool in safeguarding the authenticity and integrity of our digital interactions.

In our journey through the fascinating world of cryptography and its multifaceted applications, we arrive at a crucial domain: authentication protocols and techniques. Authentication is the process of verifying the identity of a user, device, or entity to ensure that they are who they claim to be. It's a fundamental building block of information security, forming the basis for secure access control, data protection, and trust establishment in various contexts. Imagine a scenario where you need to access your online banking account or log into your email. Authentication ensures that only authorized individuals, like you, gain access to these sensitive systems. In the realm of cryptography, authentication takes on various forms and employs a variety of protocols and techniques to achieve its objectives. One of the most common methods of authentication is the use of passwords or passphrases. This approach involves users providing a secret string of characters (the password) that, when correctly matched, grants them access. However, passwords have their limitations, such as vulnerability to brute-force attacks and susceptibility to user errors like choosing weak passwords. To enhance security, multi-factor authentication (MFA) has gained prominence. MFA combines two or more authentication factors to increase the confidence in the user's identity. The factors typically fall into three categories: something you know (e.g., a password), something you have (e.g., a mobile device or smart card), and something you are (e.g., biometric traits like fingerprints or facial recognition). This layered approach significantly bolsters security because even if one factor is compromised, others provide an additional barrier. In the realm of cryptography, one prominent authentication protocol is the Extensible Authentication Protocol (EAP). EAP is a framework that supports various authentication methods, including passwords, digital certificates, and one-time passwords. It's often used in wireless networks (WPA2/WPA3) and virtual private networks (VPNs) to establish secure connections. In addition to EAP, the Kerberos protocol plays a crucial role in authentication within a networked environment. Kerberos is widely used in Windows Active Directory domains and is known for its robust security features. It relies on a trusted third party (the Key Distribution Center or KDC) to validate the identity of users and services, reducing the risk of unauthorized access. Beyond passwords and traditional authentication methods, cryptographic techniques like digital signatures and public key cryptography play a pivotal role. Digital signatures, as we explored earlier, allow users to verify the authenticity of messages and documents. They also serve as a means of authenticating the sender, as only the holder of the private key associated with the digital signature can create it. Public key cryptography, on the other hand, enables secure key exchange and encryption of data, ensuring that only the intended recipient can decrypt and access the information. In secure communication protocols like HTTPS, public key certificates are used to authenticate the webserver, assuring users of the website's legitimacy.

Biometric authentication techniques have seen widespread adoption, particularly in mobile devices and access control systems. Biometrics relies on unique physical or behavioral traits, such as fingerprints, iris patterns, voice recognition, or facial features, to confirm a user's identity. The advantage of biometrics is the difficulty of impersonation since these traits are unique to individuals. However, biometric data needs to be securely stored and protected to prevent unauthorized access and potential misuse. Smart cards and token-based authentication are also prevalent in secure access control systems. Smart cards, often referred to as chip cards or integrated circuit cards (ICCs), contain a microprocessor and storage for cryptographic keys and credentials. When users insert a smart card into a reader and provide a PIN, the card validates their identity and provides access to secured resources. Tokens, on the other hand, generate one-time passwords or passcodes, which users input during authentication. These passcodes change periodically, making them resistant to replay attacks and enhancing security. In modern cryptographic systems, the security of authentication protocols is paramount. One must consider potential threats like eavesdropping, man-in-the-middle attacks, and replay attacks. To mitigate these threats, secure communication channels, such as Transport Layer Security (TLS) and Secure Sockets Layer (SSL), are often used. These protocols ensure that data exchanged between parties remains confidential and tamper-proof during authentication and subsequent communication. Furthermore, cryptographic techniques like challenge-response mechanisms add an extra layer of security. In a challenge-response system, a verifier issues a random challenge, and the user must provide a valid response based on a shared secret or cryptographic key. This ensures that even if an attacker intercepts the challenge, they cannot generate the correct response without knowledge of the secret. As technology continues to evolve, authentication protocols and techniques adapt to meet the demands of an increasingly interconnected and digital world. Mobile devices, for instance, leverage fingerprint and facial recognition technologies for user authentication. Blockchain technology introduces novel authentication methods, like decentralized identity management. The Internet of Things (IoT) poses unique challenges, as authentication must extend to a vast array of connected devices. In summary, authentication protocols and techniques form the bedrock of security in the digital age. Whether you're logging into your email, conducting online transactions, or accessing sensitive systems, authentication ensures that only authorized individuals gain entry. From traditional passwords to cutting-edge biometrics and cryptographic methods, authentication continuously evolves to meet the ever-changing landscape of cybersecurity.

Chapter 7: Secure Communication Protocols

In our interconnected digital world, the need for secure communication over the internet has become more critical than ever before.

Imagine the vast web of information that constitutes the internet—an intricate network of devices, servers, and users constantly exchanging data. Within this web, sensitive information flows freely, encompassing personal messages, financial transactions, medical records, and much more.

With this vast exchange of data comes the ever-present risk of unauthorized access, interception, and manipulation. It's a landscape where cybercriminals seek to exploit vulnerabilities and where safeguarding sensitive information is paramount.

Secure communication over the internet involves a set of techniques and protocols designed to protect the confidentiality, integrity, and authenticity of data exchanged between two or more parties.

At the core of secure communication lies encryption, a fundamental concept in modern cryptography. Encryption transforms plain, readable data into an unintelligible format using a mathematical algorithm and a secret key.

Imagine that you're sending a private message to a friend. Before sending it, you encrypt the message using a specific encryption algorithm and a secret key that only you and your friend possess. Once encrypted, the message appears as a jumble of characters, gibberish to anyone who intercepts it.

The true power of encryption lies in the fact that only the recipient, armed with the corresponding decryption key, can reverse the process and turn the gibberish back into the original message. In this way, encryption ensures that even if someone intercepts the communication, they can't make sense of it without the decryption key.

One of the most widely used encryption protocols for secure communication over the internet is the Transport Layer Security (TLS) protocol. You may also encounter its predecessor, the Secure Sockets Layer (SSL). These protocols establish secure, encrypted connections between web browsers and servers, ensuring that sensitive data, such as credit card information, remains confidential during online transactions.

The TLS and SSL protocols use a combination of symmetric and asymmetric encryption. Symmetric encryption, which relies on a single shared key, is used for encrypting the bulk of the data because it's faster and more efficient. Asymmetric encryption, with its pair of public and private keys, is used for secure key exchange and authentication.

Imagine you're accessing your online banking account. When you type in the web address and press enter, your web browser communicates with the bank's server using the TLS protocol. During the initial handshake, the server sends its public key to your browser. Your browser then generates a random session key, encrypts it with the server's public key, and sends it back to the server.

The server, using its private key, decrypts the session key and confirms that the browser is legitimate. Now, both your browser and the server have a shared session key that they can use for symmetric encryption during your secure session. This exchange ensures that your communication remains confidential and secure throughout your online banking session.

Secure communication over the internet extends beyond web browsers and servers. Virtual Private Networks (VPNs) are a common tool for ensuring privacy and security in various online activities, from remote work to accessing geographically restricted content.

VPNs create an encrypted tunnel through which data travels, protecting it from potential eavesdropping or censorship. When you connect to a VPN, your internet traffic is routed through a secure server, and your IP address is masked, enhancing anonymity and security.

Additionally, email communication can also benefit from secure protocols. Secure/Multipurpose Internet Mail Extensions (S/MIME) and Pretty Good Privacy (PGP) are widely used email encryption techniques that ensure the confidentiality and integrity of email messages. These methods rely on public key infrastructure (PKI) and digital signatures to verify the authenticity of messages.

As our digital world evolves, so do the threats to secure communication. Man-in-the-middle attacks, where an attacker intercepts and potentially alters communication between two parties, remain a significant concern. To mitigate this threat, protocols like TLS employ certificates issued by trusted Certificate Authorities (CAs) to confirm the identity of servers, preventing attackers from posing as legitimate websites.

It's worth noting that while encryption plays a crucial role in securing communication, it is not the sole solution. Strong authentication mechanisms, such as two-factor authentication (2FA) and biometrics, bolster security by ensuring that only authorized individuals gain access.

Moreover, constant vigilance and updates are essential in the ongoing battle against emerging threats.

Cryptographic algorithms that were once considered secure may become vulnerable as computing power advances, necessitating the adoption of more robust encryption methods.

In summary, secure communication over the internet is a cornerstone of modern life, enabling safe online transactions, private conversations, and the protection of sensitive information. It relies on encryption, authentication, and protocols like TLS, VPNs, and secure email techniques to safeguard data in an interconnected world.

As technology continues to evolve, ensuring secure communication remains a dynamic and ever-pressing challenge. Cybersecurity professionals, developers, and organizations must stay vigilant and adapt to emerging threats to keep our digital interactions safe and secure.

In the intricate realm of cryptography and information security, the preservation of confidentiality and integrity stands as an essential objective. Confidentiality pertains to the assurance that sensitive data remains hidden from unauthorized access or disclosure. Imagine you're sharing personal information with your doctor through an online portal; you trust that this data will be kept confidential, away from prying eyes.

On the other hand, integrity focuses on safeguarding the accuracy and completeness of data. In a world driven by digital transactions, think of the importance of ensuring that your financial transactions are not tampered with, and the amounts remain unchanged.

These two pillars—confidentiality and integrity—form the foundation of secure communication and data protection.

To achieve these goals, a suite of cryptographic protocols and techniques has been developed, each tailored to specific use cases and scenarios.

At the heart of these protocols lies the concept of encryption, a process that transforms data into an unreadable form using algorithms and keys. Imagine you're sending an email to your lawyer, sharing confidential legal documents. Before sending, you encrypt the email to ensure its confidentiality.

In secure communication, one widely adopted protocol is the Transport Layer Security (TLS) protocol, which works behind the scenes to provide encrypted connections between web browsers and servers. When you connect to a secure website, such as your online banking portal, TLS ensures that your communication remains confidential and tamper-proof.

TLS utilizes both symmetric and asymmetric encryption to achieve its objectives. Symmetric encryption is efficient and fast for encrypting the bulk of the data. Asymmetric encryption, with its pair of public and private keys, comes into play during the initial handshake to securely exchange encryption keys.

Imagine you're connecting to your favorite e-commerce site to make a purchase. When you enter your credit card information, TLS ensures that this data is encrypted and remains confidential as it travels over the internet.

Beyond web communication, secure email communication is another arena where confidentiality and integrity are paramount. Protocols like Pretty Good Privacy (PGP) and Secure/Multipurpose Internet Mail Extensions (S/MIME) employ encryption techniques to protect the content of email messages. Before hitting the send button on a sensitive business email, you may choose to apply PGP encryption to maintain confidentiality.

Digital signatures play a pivotal role in ensuring the integrity of digital documents and messages. Imagine you're a software developer, distributing updates for your application. To ensure that these updates are genuine and unaltered, you sign them with your digital signature.

A digital signature is created by applying a mathematical operation to a document or message using a private key. The resulting signature is specific to both the content and the private key, making it practically impossible to forge.

In a scenario like software distribution, when users receive the update, they can verify the digital signature using the corresponding public key. If the signature is valid, it confirms that the update hasn't been tampered with during transit.

Similarly, Public Key Infrastructure (PKI) is a comprehensive framework that leverages digital certificates, digital signatures, and asymmetric encryption to ensure the confidentiality and integrity of data. Imagine you're accessing your company's internal network remotely. PKI is responsible for verifying your identity and ensuring secure communication.

Within the PKI framework, Certificate Authorities (CAs) issue digital certificates to entities, validating their identity. These certificates serve as digital passports, attesting that the entity is who they claim to be.

When you access a secure website, your web browser checks the website's digital certificate, which has been issued and signed by a trusted CA. This verification process ensures that you're connecting to the legitimate website, protecting both confidentiality and integrity.

In addition to securing communication, blockchain technology introduces a novel approach to maintaining data integrity in a decentralized manner. Imagine you're part of a supply chain, and you want to ensure the integrity of product tracking information. Blockchain records and timestamps each transaction in a way that makes it tamper-evident.

In a blockchain, each block contains a cryptographic hash of the previous block, creating a chain of linked, immutable records. Once a transaction is recorded, altering any previous block would require changing all subsequent blocks, making tampering practically impossible.

Blockchain's transparency and immutability make it suitable for applications beyond cryptocurrencies, including supply chain management, voting systems, and healthcare records.

While encryption, digital signatures, and PKI are essential tools in ensuring confidentiality and integrity, the landscape of cybersecurity is continually evolving. Threats like advanced persistent threats (APTs), zero-day vulnerabilities, and insider attacks constantly challenge the security of data.

To address these threats, ongoing research and development in cryptographic protocols and techniques are crucial. Cryptography must adapt to emerging challenges and vulnerabilities, often necessitating the adoption of more robust encryption algorithms and mechanisms.

In summary, protocols for ensuring confidentiality and integrity stand as vital guardians of secure communication and data protection in our interconnected world. From web browsers to secure emails and blockchain technology, these protocols and techniques are the pillars upon which trust in digital interactions is built.

As technology evolves and the digital landscape continues to expand, the need for strong encryption, robust authentication, and data integrity will only become more critical. The ongoing pursuit of innovation in cryptography is essential to keeping data safe and maintaining the confidentiality and integrity of our digital lives.

Chapter 8: Cryptographic Hash Functions

In the realm of cryptography, one of the most versatile and essential tools is the cryptographic hash function. These functions play a crucial role in ensuring data integrity, authenticity, and security in various applications. Imagine you're uploading a file to a cloud storage service, and you want to verify that the file hasn't been tampered with during transmission.

A cryptographic hash function takes an input, also known as a message or data, and transforms it into a fixed-size string of characters, typically a sequence of numbers and letters. This output, known as the hash value or hash code, is unique to the specific input data. Even a tiny change in the input data results in a significantly different hash value.

The beauty of cryptographic hash functions lies in their properties, which make them invaluable in many cryptographic applications. One essential property is determinism, meaning that for a given input, a cryptographic hash function always produces the same hash value. Imagine you're sending a critical document to a colleague, and you both need to verify its authenticity independently. With determinism, you can be confident that you'll both compute the same hash value if the document hasn't changed.

Another crucial property is efficiency—a good cryptographic hash function computes the hash value quickly, making it suitable for real-time applications. Imagine you're logging into a secure website, and the server needs to verify your password hash promptly to grant access.

Pre-image resistance is a property that ensures it's computationally infeasible to reverse a cryptographic hash function. In other words, given a hash value, it's practically impossible to find the original input that produced it. Imagine you're storing user passwords in a database; even if an attacker gains access to the hashes, they can't easily reverse-engineer the passwords.

A strong cryptographic hash function also exhibits the avalanche effect. This means that even a minor change in the input data results in a vastly different hash value. Imagine you're digitally signing a document, and you want to ensure that even the slightest alteration to the document is detectable in the hash value.

Cryptographic hash functions are also collision-resistant, meaning that it's highly improbable for two different inputs to produce the same hash value. Imagine you're using a digital certificate to verify the authenticity of a website; collision resistance ensures that an attacker can't create a fraudulent certificate with the same hash value as the legitimate one.

Now, let's explore some common uses of cryptographic hash functions in more detail. One of the primary applications is data integrity verification. When you download a file from the internet, such as open-source software, you can verify its integrity by comparing the hash value provided by the source with the hash value computed from the downloaded file. If the two hash values match, it's highly likely that the file hasn't been tampered with during transmission.

Another critical use is in password storage. Instead of storing passwords directly in a database, systems store their hash values. When a user logs in, the system computes the hash of the entered password and compares it to the stored hash value. If they match, access is granted without the need to store the actual password, enhancing security.

Cryptographic hash functions also play a pivotal role in digital signatures. Imagine you're signing a contract electronically; your digital signature is created by applying a cryptographic hash function to the contract data. This hash value is then encrypted with your private key, creating a digital signature that can be verified using your public key. The recipient can confirm both the integrity of the document and your identity through this process.

Blockchain technology heavily relies on cryptographic hash functions. In a blockchain, each block contains a cryptographic hash of the previous block, creating a linked and tamper-evident chain of records. Changing any information in a block would necessitate altering the subsequent blocks, making tampering virtually impossible.

Cryptographic hash functions also underpin the security of digital certificates in Public Key Infrastructure (PKI). A digital certificate includes a hash value of the certificate content, signed by a trusted Certificate Authority (CA). When a web browser encounters a certificate, it can verify its authenticity by checking the hash value and the CA's digital signature.

In the realm of secure communication, cryptographic hash functions contribute to the establishment of secure connections. For example, the TLS (Transport Layer Security) protocol uses hash functions during the handshake phase to confirm the integrity of exchanged data and establish secure communication channels.

In summary, cryptographic hash functions are a cornerstone of modern cryptography, providing essential properties like determinism, efficiency, pre-image resistance, the avalanche effect, and collision resistance. Their uses span various domains, including data integrity verification, password storage, digital signatures, blockchain technology, digital certificates, and secure communication.

The cryptographic community continues to research and develop new hash functions to meet the evolving security challenges of our digital age. As technology advances and threats persist, cryptographic hash functions remain an invaluable tool for safeguarding data and ensuring the security and authenticity of digital transactions and communications.

In the vast landscape of cryptography, practical applications and security considerations stand as pillars of paramount importance. They represent the bridge between cryptographic theory and real-world implementation, where the rubber meets the road in ensuring the confidentiality, integrity, and authenticity of sensitive information.

One of the most ubiquitous and practical applications of cryptography is in securing data at rest. Imagine you're storing sensitive documents on your computer, and you want to ensure that even if someone gains access to your device, they can't read the contents. This is where encryption comes into play.

Disk encryption, like BitLocker for Windows or FileVault for macOS, encrypts the entire storage device, rendering the data unreadable without the encryption key. Even if your computer falls into the wrong hands, the data remains secure.

Similarly, mobile devices like smartphones and tablets employ encryption to protect user data. When you set a passcode or use biometric authentication, the device uses encryption to safeguard your personal information. This ensures that your photos, messages, and other data are inaccessible without the proper credentials.

Another practical application lies in secure communications over the internet. Imagine you're conducting online banking transactions or sending private messages. In these scenarios, you rely on protocols like TLS (Transport Layer Security) to establish encrypted connections between your web browser and the server.

TLS encrypts the data exchanged during the communication, shielding it from eavesdroppers and ensuring its integrity. This ensures that your sensitive information, such as credit card details or personal messages, remains confidential.

Secure email communication is another crucial application. When you send an email with sensitive content, you can encrypt it using tools like Pretty Good Privacy (PGP) or Secure/Multipurpose Internet Mail Extensions (S/MIME). These cryptographic methods ensure that only the intended recipient can decrypt and read the message.

Digital signatures are employed for document and message authentication. Imagine you're a business owner signing a contract electronically. A digital signature, created using a cryptographic hash function and your private key, verifies both the document's integrity and your identity. This ensures that the contract has not been tampered with, and your signature is genuine.

Blockchain technology leverages cryptographic principles for securing and validating transactions in a decentralized ledger. Imagine you're making a cryptocurrency payment. Blockchain's use of cryptographic hash functions and consensus mechanisms ensures the integrity and immutability of transaction records. This trustless system eliminates the need for intermediaries.

In the realm of password management, cryptographic hash functions are vital. Instead of storing plain-text passwords in a database, systems store their hash values. When you log in, the system hashes the entered password and compares it to the stored hash. This enhances security by preventing the exposure of actual passwords in case of data breaches.

Identity and access management systems rely on cryptographic authentication. Imagine you're accessing a secure network remotely. Through Public Key Infrastructure (PKI) and digital certificates, these systems verify your identity, ensuring secure and authenticated access.

However, practical applications of cryptography also come with their share of security considerations. Cryptographic systems must be robust and resilient to attacks. Imagine a determined attacker attempting to crack an encrypted message or gain unauthorized access to a system. Security vulnerabilities can expose sensitive data to malicious actors.

One significant consideration is the choice of cryptographic algorithms. Cryptographers must select algorithms that are currently secure against known attacks and have a long-term resistance to emerging threats. The transition from legacy encryption methods to more robust algorithms is a critical step in maintaining security.

Key management is another vital aspect. Imagine you're an organization managing thousands of encryption keys for various systems and applications. Proper key management practices, such as secure storage and rotation, are essential to safeguarding cryptographic systems.

Insecure key management can lead to breaches and compromise the confidentiality of sensitive data. Effective key generation, distribution, and revocation are crucial components of a secure cryptographic infrastructure.

Quantum computing poses a unique challenge to cryptographic systems. Imagine quantum computers becoming capable of breaking traditional encryption methods. To counter this threat, cryptographers are developing post-quantum cryptography, which relies on algorithms that are secure even in the face of quantum attacks.

Another security consideration is side-channel attacks. These attacks exploit unintended information leakage from cryptographic systems, such as power consumption or electromagnetic radiation. Protecting against side-channel attacks requires designing secure hardware and software implementations.

Finally, secure cryptographic practices must extend beyond technology to include human factors. Imagine an employee with access to sensitive data being targeted by social engineering. Education and awareness programs play a crucial role in mitigating these threats.

In summary, practical applications of cryptography are integral to securing our digital lives, from data storage and communication to identity management and blockchain technology. However, security considerations are paramount, and cryptographic systems must be resilient to attacks, employ robust algorithms, and implement sound key management practices.

As technology evolves and threats persist, the ongoing development and deployment of secure cryptographic solutions remain essential in safeguarding our digital interactions and protecting sensitive information.

Chapter 9: Post-Quantum Cryptography

The advent of quantum computing has ushered in a new era of technological advancements, but it also poses a formidable threat to current cryptographic systems. Imagine a future where quantum computers have the processing power to crack widely used encryption algorithms with ease. This scenario could have profound implications for data security, privacy, and the integrity of digital communication.

To understand the threat quantum computing poses, it's essential to grasp the fundamental differences between classical and quantum computers. Classical computers process information using bits, which can represent either a 0 or a 1. Quantum computers, on the other hand, leverage quantum bits or qubits, which can exist in multiple states simultaneously due to the principles of superposition.

This property of superposition enables quantum computers to perform certain calculations exponentially faster than classical computers. Imagine solving complex mathematical problems or factoring large numbers in a fraction of the time it would take classical computers. This ability could potentially break widely used encryption schemes that rely on the difficulty of factoring large numbers, such as RSA encryption.

One of the most well-known quantum algorithms with implications for cryptography is Shor's algorithm. Imagine you're encrypting data using RSA, a popular public key encryption method. The security of RSA relies on the difficulty of factoring the product of two large prime numbers. Shor's algorithm, when executed on a sufficiently powerful quantum computer, can efficiently factor large numbers, rendering RSA encryption vulnerable.

Similarly, elliptic curve cryptography (ECC), another widely used encryption technique, could be compromised by quantum computers. Imagine ECC as a digital lock that requires finding the discrete logarithm of a point on an elliptic curve—a task that's computationally infeasible for classical computers. Quantum computers, however, have the potential to solve this problem efficiently through algorithms like Grover's algorithm, posing a significant threat to ECC.

Post-quantum cryptography (PQC) is an area of ongoing research and development aimed at designing cryptographic algorithms that can withstand attacks from quantum computers. Imagine a future where PQC becomes a necessity to secure sensitive data. These algorithms rely on mathematical problems that are believed to be quantum-resistant, such as lattice-based cryptography or code-based cryptography.

Despite the looming threat, it's important to note that practical, large-scale quantum computers capable of breaking current cryptographic systems remain in the realm of theoretical research. Imagine the development of quantum computers with thousands or millions of qubits, far surpassing the capabilities of the quantum computers available today. This progress is still in its early stages and faces significant engineering and scientific challenges.

Quantum error correction is another critical area of research in quantum computing. Imagine quantum computers as highly delicate instruments that are susceptible to noise and errors. Quantum error correction seeks to address these issues and ensure the reliability of quantum computations.

One potential solution to mitigate the threat of quantum computing is quantum-resistant cryptography. Imagine a cryptographic landscape where algorithms designed to be secure against quantum attacks become the new standard.

This transition would require a concerted effort from the cybersecurity community, businesses, and governments to adopt and implement quantum-resistant cryptographic solutions.

Quantum-resistant cryptography comes with its own set of challenges and trade-offs. Imagine designing cryptographic algorithms that are both secure and efficient in a post-quantum world. Researchers must strike a delicate balance between security, performance, and practicality to ensure the widespread adoption of these solutions.

Another approach is quantum key distribution (QKD), which leverages the principles of quantum mechanics to secure communication. Imagine sending cryptographic keys between two parties using entangled photons. Any attempt to intercept the keys would disrupt the quantum state, alerting the parties to potential eavesdropping. QKD offers a promising avenue for secure communication even in a quantum-enabled world.

The timeline for the development and deployment of quantum-resistant cryptographic solutions remains uncertain. Imagine a race against time as quantum researchers work to build powerful quantum computers while cryptographic experts strive to fortify our digital defenses. The outcome of this race will shape the future of cybersecurity.

In the meantime, organizations and individuals must consider the long-term security of their sensitive data. Imagine the need to assess the lifespan of encrypted data and the potential risks posed by future quantum attacks. This strategic planning is essential to safeguarding critical information.

It's worth noting that not all encryption is equally vulnerable to quantum attacks. Imagine the importance of assessing the specific cryptographic methods in use and their susceptibility to quantum threats. A diversified approach that combines both classical and post-quantum cryptography can enhance security.

In summary, the threat of quantum computing to current cryptography is a topic of significant concern and ongoing research. Imagine a future where the security landscape is shaped by the emergence of quantum computers capable of breaking widely used encryption algorithms. While this future remains uncertain, the development of quantum-resistant cryptography and other quantum-safe solutions is crucial to ensuring the continued security of digital communication and data protection.

As quantum technology advances, the cybersecurity community must remain vigilant and proactive in adapting to the evolving threat landscape, working together to secure our digital world against the power of quantum computing.

In the ever-evolving landscape of cryptography, the emergence of quantum computing as a potential threat has catalyzed the development of post-quantum cryptographic algorithms. Imagine these algorithms as the next generation of cryptographic techniques designed to resist attacks from quantum computers, which could potentially break currently used encryption methods.

The primary motivation behind post-quantum cryptography is to ensure the long-term security of digital communication and data protection. Imagine a future where quantum computers become powerful enough to crack widely used encryption schemes, potentially compromising the confidentiality, integrity, and authenticity of sensitive information.

One of the key challenges in transitioning to post-quantum cryptography is selecting cryptographic algorithms that are both secure and practical. Imagine the importance of algorithms that can provide strong security while maintaining acceptable performance levels in real-world applications. This delicate balance is essential to ensure the widespread adoption of post-quantum cryptographic solutions.

Lattice-based cryptography is one of the leading contenders in the post-quantum cryptography arena. Imagine lattice-based cryptography as a mathematical framework that leverages the complexity of lattice problems to create secure encryption and digital signature algorithms. These algorithms are believed to be resistant to attacks by both classical and quantum computers.

Another promising approach is code-based cryptography, which relies on the difficulty of decoding random linear codes. Imagine encoding information in a way that requires solving complex mathematical problems to recover the original data. Code-based cryptography offers a high level of security and is considered a strong candidate for post-quantum cryptographic applications.

Multivariate Polynomial (MQ) cryptography is yet another approach in the post-quantum space. Imagine representing cryptographic problems as systems of multivariate polynomial equations. Solving these equations is computationally challenging and believed to be resistant to attacks by quantum computers.

Hash-based cryptography, based on the Merkle-Damgård construction, is a well-established technique that remains secure in the face of quantum computing. Imagine a cryptographic system that relies on the one-wayness of hash functions. While hash-based cryptography offers quantum resistance, it comes with certain limitations, such as key management complexities.

One of the significant challenges in transitioning to post-quantum cryptography is ensuring interoperability with existing cryptographic systems. Imagine a world where various cryptographic protocols and algorithms coexist, some designed for classical computers and others for quantum-resistant security. Efforts are underway to standardize post-quantum cryptographic algorithms to facilitate this transition.

The National Institute of Standards and Technology (NIST) in the United States has been at the forefront of this standardization effort. Imagine NIST as a central authority tasked with evaluating and selecting post-quantum cryptographic algorithms through an open and collaborative process. Their goal is to establish a set of recommended cryptographic standards that can withstand quantum attacks.

The NIST Post-Quantum Cryptography Standardization project began in 2016 and is ongoing. Imagine a rigorous evaluation process that involves cryptographic experts from around the world assessing the security and performance of candidate algorithms. The aim is to provide the cybersecurity community with a set of robust and vetted post-quantum cryptographic algorithms.

In addition to selecting secure algorithms, another critical aspect of the transition to post-quantum cryptography is the development of practical implementation strategies. Imagine the need for organizations and businesses to seamlessly integrate post-quantum cryptographic solutions into their existing systems and processes. This transition should be gradual to minimize disruptions and ensure a smooth migration.

One approach is hybrid cryptography, which combines classical and post-quantum cryptographic algorithms. Imagine a scenario where sensitive data is encrypted using both classical and post-quantum algorithms. This dual-layered approach ensures security against both quantum and classical attacks while allowing organizations to adapt gradually.

Key management plays a pivotal role in the transition. Imagine the challenge of securely generating, distributing, and storing cryptographic keys for post-quantum systems. Efficient and secure key management solutions are essential to the overall security of cryptographic implementations.

Another consideration is the cost of the transition to post-quantum cryptography. Imagine organizations investing in new hardware, software, and training to adopt quantum-resistant algorithms. Budgetary planning and resource allocation are crucial to a successful transition.

The education and awareness of cybersecurity professionals and end-users are vital components of the transition. Imagine the need for training programs and educational resources to ensure that individuals and organizations understand the implications of post-quantum cryptography and how to use these new cryptographic techniques effectively.

As the development and standardization of post-quantum cryptographic algorithms continue, organizations should consider conducting risk assessments. Imagine evaluating the potential impact of quantum computing on the security of sensitive data and communication channels. This proactive approach allows organizations to identify areas that require immediate attention and mitigation.

Ultimately, the transition to post-quantum cryptography is a collaborative effort that involves governments, businesses, researchers, and the broader cybersecurity community. Imagine a shared commitment to safeguarding digital communication and data in an era where quantum computing poses unprecedented challenges to traditional cryptographic methods.

While the timeline for the widespread adoption of post-quantum cryptography remains uncertain, the importance of preparing for this quantum-enabled future cannot be overstated. Imagine a world where our digital interactions and sensitive information remain secure, protected by the resilience of post-quantum cryptographic algorithms.

In summary, post-quantum cryptographic algorithms and transition strategies are essential components of our cybersecurity roadmap. Imagine a future where quantum-resistant encryption and digital signatures become the new standard, ensuring the long-term security of our digital world. The journey to this future is underway, guided by the collaborative efforts of experts and organizations dedicated to preserving the integrity and confidentiality of our digital lives.

Chapter 10: Implementing and Evaluating Cryptographic Systems

Implementing cryptographic systems effectively requires adherence to best practices that ensure security and reliability. Imagine a scenario where sensitive data and communication rely on cryptographic protection, making it crucial to get the implementation right.

One of the foundational principles in implementing cryptographic systems is to use well-established and vetted cryptographic algorithms. Imagine the importance of relying on algorithms that have withstood years of scrutiny and analysis by experts. This ensures that the cryptographic foundation of your system is strong and resilient.

Key management is a critical aspect of any cryptographic implementation. Imagine the keys as the digital keys to your castle; they must be generated, stored, and managed securely. Establishing robust key management practices is essential to the overall security of your system.

Generating truly random cryptographic keys is paramount. Imagine the need for keys that are unpredictable and cannot be easily guessed or derived by an attacker. Pseudo-random number generators (PRNGs) can be used to create cryptographic keys, but they should be seeded with sufficient entropy to ensure randomness.

Protecting cryptographic keys is as crucial as their generation. Imagine a scenario where an attacker gains access to your encryption keys. They could decrypt your sensitive data and compromise your security. Using hardware security modules (HSMs) or secure key storage solutions can safeguard your keys from unauthorized access.

Secure communication channels are essential for transmitting cryptographic keys. Imagine the risk of eavesdropping during the key exchange process. Protocols like Transport Layer Security (TLS) ensure that key exchange happens securely, protecting your communication from interception.

Regularly updating and rotating keys is a good practice. Imagine the impact of using the same cryptographic key for an extended period. If the key becomes compromised, all data encrypted with it is at risk. By periodically changing keys, you minimize the potential damage of a key breach.

Cryptographic systems should be configured with strong security parameters. Imagine using weak encryption algorithms or short key lengths. These vulnerabilities can be exploited by attackers, compromising the security of your system. Always follow industry best practices for cryptographic parameter selection.

Secure your system against side-channel attacks. Imagine an attacker analyzing the power consumption or electromagnetic radiation of your device to deduce cryptographic keys. Countermeasures like masking, blinding, and implementing secure hardware can protect against such attacks.

Regularly updating cryptographic libraries and software is essential. Imagine the discovery of vulnerabilities or weaknesses in cryptographic algorithms or implementations. Patching these issues promptly ensures that your system remains secure.

Testing and auditing your cryptographic implementations are crucial steps. Imagine assuming your system is secure without rigorous testing. Thoroughly evaluate your cryptographic systems for vulnerabilities, and consider third-party security audits to identify potential weaknesses.

Implementing proper access controls is fundamental. Imagine unauthorized personnel gaining access to cryptographic keys or sensitive data. Role-based access controls and authentication mechanisms help restrict access to authorized individuals.

Maintain a strong focus on secure coding practices. Imagine vulnerabilities introduced due to coding errors. Training your development team in secure coding techniques can prevent common security issues.

When dealing with cryptographic keys, consider using multi-factor authentication. Imagine the added layer of security when users must provide something they know (a password) and something they have (a cryptographic key). This approach enhances access control and protects against unauthorized use.

Implement secure update mechanisms for your cryptographic systems. Imagine an attacker compromising your system by injecting malicious updates. Ensure that only authorized and authenticated updates can be applied to your system.

Regularly monitor and audit your cryptographic systems for signs of intrusion or suspicious activity. Imagine the importance of detecting and responding to security incidents promptly. Implementing intrusion detection systems and monitoring tools can help identify potential threats.

Ensure that you have a well-defined incident response plan in place. Imagine a security breach occurring despite your best efforts. Having a plan to contain and mitigate the damage is essential for minimizing the impact of security incidents.

Secure communication between components of your cryptographic system. Imagine the risk of attackers intercepting data as it moves between different parts of your system. Encrypting data in transit and ensuring the integrity of communication channels is crucial.

Stay informed about the latest developments in cryptography and security. Imagine the ever-evolving nature of security threats. Regularly update your knowledge and practices to adapt to emerging threats and vulnerabilities.

Consider the implications of quantum computing for your cryptographic systems. Imagine a future where quantum computers could break existing encryption. Exploring post-quantum cryptography and planning for a quantum-secure future is prudent.

Finally, document your cryptographic system's design, implementation, and operational procedures. Imagine the need to troubleshoot issues or transfer knowledge to new team members. Comprehensive documentation ensures the continuity and maintainability of your cryptographic systems.

In summary, implementing cryptographic systems effectively involves a combination of best practices, rigorous testing, and a proactive approach to security. Imagine a robust defense against potential threats, where cryptographic implementations are well-prepared to protect your sensitive data and communication. By following these best practices, you can fortify your cryptographic systems and navigate the complex landscape of digital security with confidence.

Evaluating the security and performance of cryptographic implementations is a critical aspect of ensuring the effectiveness of your security measures. Imagine it as a crucial step in the journey towards safeguarding your sensitive data and communications.

Security evaluations focus on assessing the resilience of your cryptographic system against a wide range of threats. Imagine a system that can withstand attacks by determined adversaries, from eavesdropping to brute force attacks.

Understanding the security of your implementation is fundamental to maintaining trust in your digital environment.

One common method for evaluating security is through cryptographic algorithm analysis. Imagine experts scrutinizing the underlying mathematical foundations of your chosen algorithms. This analysis aims to identify vulnerabilities, weaknesses, or potential attack vectors that could compromise your security.

Threat modeling is another valuable technique for security evaluation. Imagine a comprehensive assessment of potential threats and vulnerabilities specific to your cryptographic system. By identifying these threats early, you can proactively implement countermeasures to mitigate risks.

Penetration testing, often referred to as ethical hacking, involves attempting to exploit vulnerabilities in your system to assess its security. Imagine skilled professionals simulating real-world attacks to uncover weaknesses in your implementation. This process provides valuable insights into areas that require improvement.

Code reviews play a vital role in security evaluations. Imagine experts examining the source code of your cryptographic software for coding errors or security vulnerabilities. Thorough code reviews can identify issues that might not be apparent through other methods.

Security assessments should consider not only the cryptographic algorithms but also the overall system architecture. Imagine evaluating the security of the entire system, including key management, access control, and communication protocols. Weaknesses in any of these components can compromise the security of the entire system.

Performance evaluation is equally important in ensuring that your cryptographic system meets its operational requirements. Imagine a system that not only provides strong security but also operates efficiently and meets user expectations.

One key performance metric is processing speed. Imagine a cryptographic implementation that can encrypt and decrypt data quickly without causing significant delays. This is especially critical in applications where real-time or low-latency processing is essential.

Another performance consideration is memory usage. Imagine a cryptographic system that consumes excessive memory, potentially affecting the overall performance of your application. Efficient memory management is essential to ensure optimal system operation.

Resource consumption, including CPU utilization, should also be evaluated. Imagine the impact of a cryptographic system that places a heavy burden on your hardware resources. Efficient algorithms and implementations minimize resource usage while maintaining security.

Throughput and latency are essential performance metrics. Imagine an application that can handle a high volume of cryptographic operations while maintaining low response times. Evaluating these metrics helps ensure that your system can scale to meet increasing demand.

Scalability is crucial in performance evaluations. Imagine your cryptographic system being used in a growing organization or platform. Evaluating how well it scales and adapts to increased workloads is essential for long-term success.

Consider the impact of parallelism on performance. Imagine a system that can take advantage of multi-core processors or distributed computing environments. Efficient parallel processing can significantly enhance the performance of cryptographic operations.

Latency, especially in communication protocols, can affect the user experience. Imagine secure messaging or online transactions where excessive latency leads to delays. Evaluating and optimizing the latency of cryptographic operations is vital in such scenarios.

Energy efficiency is a growing concern in modern computing. Imagine mobile devices or IoT sensors that rely on efficient cryptographic operations to conserve battery life. Evaluating the energy consumption of your cryptographic system is essential for sustainable and environmentally friendly applications.

Performance evaluations should consider the trade-offs between security and speed. Imagine finding the right balance between strong security measures and acceptable performance levels. Customizing cryptographic implementations to meet specific use case requirements is a delicate art.

Benchmarking is a valuable technique for performance evaluation. Imagine comparing your cryptographic system's performance against industry standards or similar implementations. Benchmarking provides objective data to assess the efficiency of your implementation.

Real-world testing is essential to performance evaluations. Imagine simulating the actual operational conditions your cryptographic system will encounter. This can reveal performance bottlenecks and help you fine-tune your implementation.

User experience is a critical aspect of performance evaluations. Imagine the frustration of users dealing with a slow or unresponsive application. Ensuring that cryptographic operations do not negatively impact the user experience is essential for user satisfaction.

Security and performance evaluations often go hand in hand. Imagine a cryptographic implementation that excels in security but falls short in terms of performance. Balancing these two aspects is a complex but necessary task.

Ultimately, the evaluation of cryptographic implementations is an ongoing process. Imagine the ever-evolving landscape of security threats and performance requirements. Regularly revisiting and reassessing your cryptographic systems ensures that they remain effective and resilient.

In summary, evaluating the security and performance of cryptographic implementations is a multifaceted process that requires a thorough understanding of both security principles and performance metrics. Imagine it as a continuous journey towards achieving the right balance between strong security measures and efficient operation. By conducting these evaluations systematically, you can maintain the trust of users and stakeholders while effectively safeguarding your digital assets.

BOOK 3
ADVANCED CRYPTANALYSIS
BREAKING CODES AND CIPHERS

ROB BOTWRIGHT

Chapter 1: Understanding Cryptanalysis

Cryptanalysis, often referred to as the art of codebreaking, plays a vital role in the field of cryptography. Imagine it as the counterbalance to encryption, a process that seeks to uncover hidden information and vulnerabilities within cryptographic systems.

The primary objective of cryptanalysis is to analyze and decipher encrypted messages without access to the decryption key. Imagine the challenge of decrypting a message that was designed to be unintelligible without the proper key. Cryptanalysts employ various techniques and strategies to achieve this goal.

One of the fundamental methods in cryptanalysis is frequency analysis. Imagine analyzing the frequency of letters, symbols, or patterns within an encrypted message. In languages with predictable letter frequencies, this method can help deduce the encryption key or decipher the message.

Cryptanalysts often rely on known plaintext or ciphertext attacks. Imagine having access to both the encrypted message and the corresponding plaintext. By studying the relationship between the two, cryptanalysts can uncover patterns and vulnerabilities in the encryption process.

Chosen plaintext attacks involve sending specific plaintexts to be encrypted and analyzing the corresponding ciphertext. Imagine the value of having control over the plaintext inputs. This method allows cryptanalysts to gain insights into the encryption algorithm and potentially discover weaknesses.

Differential cryptanalysis is a powerful technique used to analyze the differences between pairs of plaintexts and their corresponding ciphertexts. Imagine comparing how slight changes in the input data affect the output. Cryptanalysts can use this method to identify patterns and weaknesses in cryptographic algorithms.

Linear cryptanalysis focuses on finding linear relationships between plaintext, ciphertext, and the encryption key. Imagine mathematical equations that describe these relationships. Cryptanalysts use linear cryptanalysis to derive information about the key or algorithm.

Brute force attacks are perhaps the most straightforward method of cryptanalysis. Imagine systematically trying every possible key until the correct one is found. While this method can be time-consuming, it is effective when all other avenues of attack are exhausted.

Cryptanalysis also involves studying the properties of cryptographic algorithms themselves. Imagine examining the mathematical foundations and computational complexity of encryption algorithms. This analysis can reveal vulnerabilities that may not be apparent through other means.

Side-channel attacks are a unique form of cryptanalysis that target the physical implementation of cryptographic systems. Imagine analyzing factors such as power consumption, electromagnetic radiation, or timing variations during cryptographic operations. These subtle signals can provide insights into the encryption process and potentially lead to key recovery.

Quantum cryptanalysis is a relatively new field that explores the potential impact of quantum computers on cryptography. Imagine the immense computing power of quantum machines. Cryptanalysts are researching algorithms that could break current encryption methods, highlighting the need for quantum-resistant cryptography. Cryptanalysis also plays a crucial role in assessing the security of cryptographic protocols. Imagine the complexity of protocols used in secure communication, such as SSL/TLS. Cryptanalysts examine these protocols for vulnerabilities that could be exploited by attackers.

In addition to breaking encryption, cryptanalysis serves another critical purpose—strengthening security. Imagine the scenario where a cryptanalyst discovers a vulnerability in an encryption algorithm. This discovery can lead to improvements in the algorithm's design, making it more resistant to attacks.

Cryptanalysts contribute to the development of secure cryptographic standards. Imagine the importance of having well-vetted encryption standards that protect sensitive information. Cryptanalysts participate in the evaluation and selection of encryption algorithms for various applications.

They also conduct security audits to identify vulnerabilities in cryptographic systems and software. Imagine the peace of mind knowing that experts are actively seeking and addressing potential weaknesses. Security audits help ensure that cryptographic implementations remain robust against evolving threats.

Cryptanalysis encourages continuous research and innovation in cryptography. Imagine the ever-evolving landscape of security threats and computational capabilities. Cryptanalysts and cryptographers engage in a perpetual cat-and-mouse game, with each side pushing the boundaries of their respective fields.

Cryptanalysis is not limited to malicious purposes; it also serves legitimate security interests. Imagine the need to verify the security of encryption methods used to protect critical infrastructure or government communications. Cryptanalysts work to ensure that these systems remain resilient against sophisticated attacks.

In summary, cryptanalysis is an essential component of the cryptographic ecosystem. Imagine it as the force that tests and refines the armor of encryption. Cryptanalysts, through their tireless efforts, strengthen our digital defenses, uncover vulnerabilities, and contribute to the ongoing pursuit of secure communication and data protection.

Cryptanalysis, the art of deciphering encrypted messages, encompasses various methods and approaches that cryptanalysts employ to break codes and ciphers. Imagine it as a puzzle-solving adventure where the goal is to unveil hidden information.

One common method used in cryptanalysis is frequency analysis. Imagine analyzing the frequency of letters or symbols within an encrypted message. This method is particularly effective in languages where certain letters or symbols appear more frequently than others.

Cryptanalysts often leverage known plaintext or ciphertext attacks. Imagine having access to both the original message and its encrypted counterpart. By comparing the two, cryptanalysts can uncover patterns and vulnerabilities in the encryption process.

Chosen plaintext attacks involve sending specific messages to be encrypted and analyzing the corresponding ciphertext. Imagine having control over the input data that is encrypted. This method allows cryptanalysts to gain insights into the encryption algorithm and potentially discover weaknesses.

Differential cryptanalysis is a powerful technique used to analyze the differences between pairs of plaintexts and their corresponding ciphertexts. Imagine studying how small changes in the input data affect the output. Cryptanalysts can use this method to identify patterns and vulnerabilities in cryptographic algorithms.

Linear cryptanalysis focuses on finding linear relationships between plaintext, ciphertext, and the encryption key. Imagine mathematical equations that describe these relationships. Cryptanalysts use linear cryptanalysis to deduce information about the key or algorithm.

Brute force attacks, while straightforward, can be effective. Imagine trying every possible key until the correct one is found. This method can be time-consuming, especially for strong encryption, but it guarantees success eventually.

Cryptanalysis also involves analyzing the mathematical properties of cryptographic algorithms. Imagine delving into the underlying mathematics and computational complexity of encryption algorithms. This analysis can reveal vulnerabilities that may not be apparent through other means.

Side-channel attacks are a unique form of cryptanalysis that target the physical implementation of cryptographic systems. Imagine analyzing factors like power consumption, electromagnetic radiation, or timing variations during cryptographic operations. These subtle signals can provide insights into the encryption process and potentially lead to key recovery.

Quantum cryptanalysis is an emerging field that explores the impact of quantum computers on cryptography. Imagine the extraordinary computing power of quantum machines. Cryptanalysts are researching algorithms that could potentially break current encryption methods, highlighting the need for quantum-resistant cryptography. Cryptanalysis is not solely about breaking encryption—it also plays a role in strengthening security. Imagine a cryptanalyst discovering a vulnerability in an encryption algorithm. This discovery can lead to improvements in the algorithm's design, making it more resistant to attacks.

Cryptanalysts contribute to the development of secure cryptographic standards. Imagine the importance of having well-vetted encryption standards that protect sensitive information. Cryptanalysts participate in evaluating and selecting encryption algorithms for various applications.

They also conduct security audits to identify vulnerabilities in cryptographic systems and software. Imagine the reassurance of knowing that experts actively seek and address potential weaknesses. Security audits help ensure that cryptographic implementations remain robust against evolving threats.

Cryptanalysis encourages ongoing research and innovation in cryptography. Imagine the ever-evolving landscape of security threats and computational capabilities. Cryptanalysts and cryptographers engage in a perpetual cat-and-mouse game, pushing the boundaries of their fields.

Cryptanalysis isn't limited to malicious purposes; it also serves legitimate security interests. Imagine the need to verify the security of encryption methods used to protect critical infrastructure or government communications. Cryptanalysts work to ensure that these systems remain resilient against sophisticated attacks.

In summary, cryptanalysis is an essential part of the cryptographic world. Imagine it as the relentless pursuit of unraveling secrets and strengthening defenses. Cryptanalysts, through their dedication and expertise, enhance our understanding of security, uncover vulnerabilities, and contribute to the ongoing quest for secure communication and data protection.

Chapter 2: Historical Cryptanalysis Techniques

Exploring the fascinating history of cryptanalysis reveals a world of intrigue and intellectual challenge. Imagine being a cryptanalyst in ancient times, faced with the task of deciphering secret messages.

One of the earliest known instances of cryptanalysis dates back to ancient Egypt. Imagine deciphering hieroglyphic inscriptions, attempting to unravel their hidden meanings. While not traditional encryption, the ancient Egyptians employed various symbolic and substitution methods to protect their messages.

The Greeks were also early pioneers in the field of cryptanalysis. Imagine being tasked with cracking the Spartan scytale, a cylinder with a strip of parchment wrapped around it. Deciphering the message required finding the correct diameter for the cylinder—a task that demanded ingenuity.

In the famous case of Julius Caesar, cryptanalysis played a role in uncovering the Caesar cipher. Imagine encountering a message where each letter is shifted by a fixed number of positions in the alphabet. This simple substitution cipher was named after the Roman general and remains a classic example.

The Arab scholar Al-Kindi, in the ninth century, made significant contributions to cryptanalysis. Imagine working with Arabic manuscripts containing encrypted messages. Al-Kindi documented techniques for frequency analysis and letter frequency distribution, laying the foundation for future cryptanalysts.

During the Renaissance, cryptanalysis gained momentum. Imagine the challenge of breaking the Vigenère cipher, a polyalphabetic substitution cipher. This cipher used a keyword to determine the shift for each letter, making it more complex than simple substitution ciphers.

The pioneering work of Blaise de Vigenère and his contemporaries added complexity to cryptographic systems. Imagine the excitement of cryptanalysts discovering ways to analyze and break these advanced ciphers. Vigenère himself developed methods to enhance the security of his cipher, showcasing the ongoing battle between encryption and cryptanalysis.

The advent of the telegraph brought new challenges to cryptanalysis. Imagine intercepting Morse code messages and deciphering the dots and dashes. Cryptanalysts developed techniques to analyze the timing and patterns of Morse code transmissions.

The famous cryptanalyst Elizebeth Friedman made significant contributions during World War II. Imagine being tasked with decrypting messages encrypted using the Enigma machine. Friedman's work was instrumental in breaking the German code, a crucial achievement in the war effort.

The development of electromechanical machines, such as the Polish Bomba and the British Bombe, marked a milestone in cryptanalysis. Imagine working with these early computers, designed to assist in decrypting complex ciphers. These machines revolutionized cryptanalysis and paved the way for modern computing.

Cryptanalysis faced a new frontier during the Cold War with the advent of computer-based encryption. Imagine the race to decipher encrypted communications between superpowers. Cryptanalysts developed methods to break these encrypted messages, contributing to the intelligence efforts of the era.

The field of cryptanalysis continued to evolve with the rise of digital encryption. Imagine decrypting messages encrypted using complex algorithms and keys. Modern cryptanalysts utilize computational power and mathematical techniques to tackle these challenges.

In recent years, cryptanalysis has expanded its scope to address emerging technologies. Imagine the complexities of analyzing encryption methods used in secure communication and data protection. Cryptanalysts play a crucial role in ensuring the security of digital systems and information.

Cryptanalysis is not solely about breaking codes—it also contributes to the development of stronger encryption. Imagine cryptanalysts identifying vulnerabilities in encryption algorithms, leading to improvements in security. This ongoing cycle of analysis and improvement is essential for maintaining the integrity of cryptographic systems.

Cryptanalysis is a dynamic field, shaped by historical developments and technological advancements. Imagine the continuous pursuit of unraveling secrets and strengthening digital defenses. Cryptanalysts, both past and present, have made invaluable contributions to the world of cryptography and information security.

In summary, the history of cryptanalysis is a testament to human ingenuity and perseverance. Imagine the challenges and triumphs of those who have dedicated their lives to deciphering encrypted messages. Their efforts have not only shaped the course of history but continue to play a vital role in the security of our digital world.

Exploring the world of famous cryptanalysis breakthroughs provides insight into the remarkable achievements of cryptanalysts throughout history. Imagine the thrill of cracking complex codes and revealing hidden messages.

One of the most iconic breakthroughs in cryptanalysis is the decipherment of the Rosetta Stone. Imagine deciphering ancient Egyptian hieroglyphs through the inscriptions on this historic artifact. The discovery of the Rosetta Stone in 1799 by Napoleon's troops eventually led to the understanding of Egyptian hieroglyphs and opened a window into ancient history.

In World War II, British cryptanalysts achieved a significant breakthrough by decoding the German Enigma machine. Imagine the moment when Alan Turing and his team cracked the Enigma code, a pivotal event in the war. Their work at Bletchley Park helped the Allies gain valuable intelligence and hastened the end of the conflict.

Cryptanalyst William Friedman made a groundbreaking contribution with his work on the Riverbank Publications. Imagine the dedication required to analyze and decipher various enciphered texts. Friedman's research laid the foundation for modern cryptanalysis techniques and set new standards for the field.

During the Cold War, the Venona project marked a crucial cryptanalysis breakthrough. Imagine uncovering Soviet espionage activities through intercepted messages. Cryptanalysts decrypted encrypted Soviet cables, revealing the extent of espionage during the Cold War and leading to the identification of spies.

In the realm of computer security, the discovery of the Stuxnet worm was a significant cryptanalysis achievement. Imagine unraveling the code behind a highly sophisticated cyberweapon. Stuxnet was designed to disrupt Iran's nuclear program, and its discovery shed light on the potential of cyber-physical attacks.

The RSA encryption algorithm has a storied history of cryptanalysis efforts. Imagine the challenge of breaking the RSA encryption, which relies on the difficulty of factoring large numbers. Cryptanalysts continuously test the security of RSA, contributing to its evolution and strength.

The cryptographic community celebrated the discovery of the SHA-1 collision vulnerability. Imagine the excitement of cryptanalysts who successfully generated two different inputs producing the same SHA-1 hash. This discovery led to the deprecation of SHA-1 in favor of more secure hash functions.

The cryptanalysis breakthroughs in quantum-resistant cryptography are of paramount importance. Imagine the race to develop encryption methods resistant to quantum attacks. Cryptanalysts work to ensure that our digital infrastructure remains secure in the face of future quantum computing capabilities.

Cryptanalysis is not limited to government agencies or elite organizations; individuals have also made remarkable breakthroughs. Imagine the dedication of amateur cryptanalysts who contribute to the field. Their passion and curiosity drive them to tackle challenging ciphers and encryption methods.

In recent years, cryptanalysts have focused on analyzing encryption used in digital currencies like Bitcoin. Imagine deciphering the intricacies of blockchain technology and cryptographic signatures. Cryptanalysts play a role in uncovering vulnerabilities and ensuring the security of cryptocurrency transactions.

The study of historical ciphers and their cryptanalysis is a rich field of research. Imagine decrypting messages from the past, shedding light on historical events and secrets. Cryptanalysts contribute to our understanding of history through their work with ancient codes and ciphers.

Modern cryptanalysis involves tackling encryption used in everyday communication and data protection. Imagine the complexity of breaking encrypted messages sent over the internet. Cryptanalysts use mathematical techniques, computational power, and advanced algorithms to address these challenges.

Cryptanalysis is an ever-evolving field, adapting to technological advancements and emerging threats. Imagine the ongoing efforts of cryptanalysts to stay ahead of adversaries and secure digital communication. Their work is essential for safeguarding sensitive information in the digital age.

Cryptanalysts are not just codebreakers; they are also guardians of security. Imagine the responsibility of ensuring that encryption methods are robust and resilient. Their contributions to strengthening cryptographic systems protect individuals, organizations, and nations.

In summary, famous cryptanalysis breakthroughs have shaped the course of history and continue to play a vital role in our digital world. Imagine a world without cryptanalysts— a world where secrets remain locked and vulnerabilities unaddressed. Their dedication, ingenuity, and perseverance underscore the importance of cryptanalysis in the realm of security and information protection.

Chapter 3: Frequency Analysis and Classical Ciphers

Frequency analysis is a fundamental technique in the field of cryptanalysis. Imagine it as a detective tool used to crack secret codes and uncover hidden messages.

At its core, frequency analysis relies on the analysis of character or symbol frequencies within a ciphertext. Imagine you have a mysterious encrypted message, and you suspect it was created using a simple substitution cipher. Frequency analysis helps you identify patterns in the ciphertext and reveal the original message.

The concept behind frequency analysis is straightforward. Imagine you're analyzing a piece of text, and you notice that certain letters or symbols appear more frequently than others. In English, for instance, the letter 'E' is the most common, followed by 'T,' 'A,' 'O,' and 'I.'

These patterns emerge because languages have characteristic letter frequencies. Imagine the excitement of discovering that these patterns can be applied to cryptanalysis. The frequencies of letters and symbols in a language can potentially expose the underlying code.

Frequency analysis was famously used to break the Caesar cipher. Imagine having a ciphertext where each letter is shifted by a fixed number of positions in the alphabet. Frequency analysis helped cryptanalysts identify the most common letter in the ciphertext, which likely corresponded to 'E' in the plaintext.

Cryptanalysts then looked for other frequent letters to decipher the shift value. Imagine the satisfaction of successfully decoding the message using frequency analysis. This breakthrough paved the way for more advanced cryptanalysis techniques.

Frequency analysis extends beyond single-letter frequencies. Imagine analyzing two-letter combinations, known as digrams, or three-letter combinations, called trigraphs. In English, 'TH' is a common digram, and 'THE' is a frequent trigraph.

Cryptanalysts use these insights to identify potential words or phrases in the ciphertext. Imagine piecing together parts of the message like a jigsaw puzzle. Frequency analysis helps uncover the hidden narrative within encrypted texts.

The effectiveness of frequency analysis depends on the length of the ciphertext. Imagine having a short message with limited character occurrences. In such cases, the analysis may not yield conclusive results.

However, longer ciphertexts are more amenable to frequency analysis. Imagine working with a substantial body of encrypted text, where statistical patterns become more pronounced. Cryptanalysts can confidently apply frequency analysis to decipher longer messages.

Language-specific frequency data is a valuable resource for cryptanalysts. Imagine having access to frequency tables that outline the likelihood of each letter's occurrence in a particular language. These tables serve as a reference for frequency analysis.

Frequency analysis can be applied to various types of codes and ciphers. Imagine working with historical manuscripts containing encrypted messages. Cryptanalysts use frequency analysis to crack centuries-old codes and uncover historical secrets.

In modern cryptography, frequency analysis is a valuable tool for cryptanalysts and penetration testers. Imagine assessing the security of an encryption system by analyzing the frequency distribution of ciphertext characters. Identifying deviations from expected patterns can reveal vulnerabilities.

Cryptanalysts often encounter challenges when dealing with more complex encryption methods. Imagine facing a ciphertext generated using a complex algorithm that disrupts the natural frequency distribution of characters. In such cases, frequency analysis may be less effective, and other techniques must be employed.

Frequency analysis is not limited to letters and symbols. Imagine the world of digital communication, where binary code is used. Cryptanalysts adapt frequency analysis to analyze the distribution of '0s' and '1s' in binary data.

Frequency analysis can also be applied to identify patterns in numerical data. Imagine decrypting encrypted financial transactions or sensitive numerical information. Cryptanalysts use frequency analysis to gain insights into the underlying data.

In summary, frequency analysis is a powerful cryptanalysis technique that hinges on the analysis of character or symbol frequencies within a ciphertext. Imagine it as a cipher-breaking detective's tool, capable of unraveling encrypted messages and uncovering hidden meanings. While it may not be effective against all encryption methods, its historical significance and continued relevance in modern cryptanalysis underscore its importance in the world of cryptography.

Cryptanalysis of classical ciphers is like solving puzzles from the past. Imagine diving into the world of secret messages and codes, deciphering the techniques used by cryptographers of bygone eras.

One of the most iconic classical ciphers is the Caesar cipher. Imagine Julius Caesar using this cipher to communicate securely with his generals. Cryptanalysis of the Caesar cipher involves exploring letter frequency patterns and conducting brute-force attacks to reveal the shift value.

Frequency analysis plays a crucial role in breaking classical ciphers. Imagine analyzing the frequency of letters in a ciphertext, hoping to find clues that lead to decryption. This method was instrumental in breaking many historical ciphers.

Another classical cipher is the Atbash cipher. Imagine reversing the alphabet so that 'A' becomes 'Z,' 'B' becomes 'Y,' and so on. Cryptanalysis of the Atbash cipher is relatively simple, as it involves a direct letter-to-letter substitution.

The Vigenère cipher adds complexity by using a keyword for encryption. Imagine having a keyword like "KEY" to encrypt a message. Cryptanalysis requires determining the keyword's length and then solving multiple Caesar ciphers with different shift values.

Frequency analysis helps identify the keyword's length. Imagine using trial and error to find a repeating pattern in the ciphertext. Once the keyword length is known, cryptanalysts can focus on deciphering the message.

The Playfair cipher introduces a grid-based approach. Imagine encrypting pairs of letters using a matrix filled with the alphabet. Cryptanalysis of the Playfair cipher involves understanding the rules for handling duplicate letters and finding the key matrix.

Breaking the Playfair cipher requires analyzing the ciphertext for pairs of letters that follow specific rules. Imagine decoding words by examining how they were encrypted in the grid. This method can be time-consuming but effective in revealing the hidden message.

The Rail Fence cipher is a transposition cipher. Imagine writing a message in a zigzag pattern and then reading it row by row. Cryptanalysis involves determining the number of rails and rearranging the letters to reveal the plaintext.

Frequency analysis is less useful for transposition ciphers like the Rail Fence. Imagine trying to apply letter frequency patterns to a message that has been rearranged. Cryptanalysts must recognize the pattern used for encryption and reverse it.

The simple substitution cipher is a straightforward letter-to-letter mapping. Imagine replacing 'A' with 'X,' 'B' with 'Y,' and so on. Cryptanalysis of simple substitution ciphers relies on recognizing common words and patterns in the ciphertext.

Frequency analysis can be effective for simple substitution ciphers. Imagine identifying frequently occurring letters and guessing their corresponding plaintext letters. Cryptanalysts use their knowledge of language to make educated guesses.

The cryptanalysis of classical ciphers often involves leveraging linguistic knowledge. Imagine using linguistic clues like common letter pairs ('TH' or 'QU') to decrypt messages. Cryptanalysts combine language expertise with cryptographic techniques.

Cryptanalysis can be a blend of art and science. Imagine the satisfaction of unraveling a centuries-old secret using a combination of analytical skills and historical context. Cryptanalysts become detectives of the past, deciphering messages left behind by people long gone.

Breaking classical ciphers is a rewarding challenge. Imagine the excitement of solving puzzles that have stumped scholars and historians for generations. Cryptanalysts feel a connection to the past as they decode messages from different historical periods.

Cryptanalysis extends beyond historical ciphers. Imagine tackling modern encryption systems used for secure communication and data protection. Cryptanalysts are at the forefront of cybersecurity, testing the resilience of encryption methods.

Today's cryptanalysts employ advanced computational techniques. Imagine using supercomputers to perform brute-force attacks on complex ciphers. Cryptanalysis has evolved with technology, becoming a critical component of digital security.

In summary, cryptanalysis of classical ciphers allows us to peer into the secrets of the past and uncover the techniques used by ancient cryptographers. Imagine it as a journey through history, where each cipher represents a unique challenge waiting to be solved. Cryptanalysts, armed with a blend of analytical skills, linguistic knowledge, and modern technology, continue to unravel the mysteries hidden within these classical codes.

Chapter 4: Modern Cryptanalysis Tools and Methods

Contemporary cryptanalysis approaches are a testament to the ongoing battle between cryptographers and those seeking to break cryptographic systems. Imagine this battle as a continuous game of cat and mouse, where new encryption methods emerge, and cryptanalysts develop innovative techniques to unravel them.

One contemporary cryptanalysis approach involves leveraging the power of computational brute force. Imagine trying every possible decryption key until the correct one is found. This method is particularly effective against weak encryption schemes with short keys.

In the world of modern cryptography, encryption keys can be extremely long and complex. Imagine attempting to crack a 256-bit AES encryption key through brute force. The number of possible keys is astronomical, making it computationally infeasible to break the encryption in a reasonable timeframe.

To address this challenge, cryptanalysts may resort to specialized hardware or distributed computing networks. Imagine harnessing the collective processing power of thousands of computers to speed up the brute-force attack. This approach is known as distributed computing or parallel processing.

Another contemporary cryptanalysis technique is the use of rainbow tables. Imagine these tables as precomputed dictionaries that map plaintexts to their corresponding ciphertexts. Cryptanalysts can use rainbow tables to quickly look up ciphertexts and discover their corresponding plaintexts.

To counteract rainbow table attacks, cryptographic systems introduce salting. Imagine adding a unique random value, called a salt, to each plaintext before encryption. This ensures that even identical plaintexts result in different ciphertexts, thwarting rainbow table attacks.

Cryptanalysts often focus on identifying vulnerabilities in the cryptographic implementation rather than attacking the encryption algorithm itself. Imagine discovering a flaw in the way encryption keys are generated or managed in a software application. Exploiting such vulnerabilities can lead to cryptographic compromises.

Side-channel attacks are a fascinating and powerful cryptanalysis approach. Imagine analyzing the physical properties of a cryptographic device, such as its power consumption or electromagnetic radiation. These subtle cues can reveal information about the encryption key or plaintext being processed.

For example, power analysis attacks involve measuring the power consumption of a device during cryptographic operations. Imagine detecting patterns in power consumption that correlate with specific calculations. This information can be used to deduce the encryption key or plaintext.

Fault injection attacks are another intriguing cryptanalysis technique. Imagine introducing intentional faults, such as voltage spikes or electromagnetic interference, into a cryptographic device. These faults can disrupt the encryption process, potentially revealing sensitive information.

Cryptanalysts also explore mathematical attacks, which target the underlying mathematics of cryptographic algorithms. Imagine finding weaknesses in the mathematical properties of encryption algorithms. These vulnerabilities can lead to more efficient attacks on the encryption.

For example, researchers have developed attacks on certain elliptic curve cryptography implementations by exploiting weaknesses in the curve parameters. Imagine manipulating these parameters to make the cryptographic calculations more predictable. This can facilitate the recovery of encryption keys.

Cryptanalysis techniques are not limited to encryption alone; they also encompass attacks on digital signatures. Imagine forging a digital signature by finding a collision in the underlying hash function. Such collisions can undermine the trustworthiness of digital signatures.

Quantum cryptanalysis is a rapidly evolving field with the potential to disrupt traditional cryptographic systems. Imagine quantum computers with the capability to perform certain calculations exponentially faster than classical computers. These quantum machines could break widely used encryption methods.

Shor's algorithm, for instance, threatens the security of RSA and other factorization-based encryption schemes. Imagine a quantum computer factoring large numbers effortlessly, rendering RSA encryption obsolete. This scenario highlights the urgency of developing quantum-resistant encryption algorithms.

Post-quantum cryptography is the response to the quantum threat. Imagine a new generation of cryptographic algorithms designed to withstand attacks from quantum computers. Cryptanalysts play a crucial role in evaluating the security of these post-quantum schemes.

Cryptanalysis is an ever-evolving field that adapts to changes in technology and the threat landscape. Imagine cryptanalysts as digital detectives, constantly exploring new methods and techniques to break encryption and improve security. Their work serves as a counterbalance to the ever-advancing world of cryptography.

In the age of the Internet of Things (IoT) and connected devices, the importance of cryptanalysis cannot be overstated. Imagine securing billions of IoT devices, each with its unique cryptographic challenges. Cryptanalysts are at the forefront of ensuring the security of these interconnected systems.

In summary, contemporary cryptanalysis approaches encompass a wide range of techniques, from brute force and rainbow tables to side-channel attacks and mathematical vulnerabilities. Imagine cryptanalysts as guardians of digital security, working diligently to uncover weaknesses in cryptographic systems and protect sensitive information. Their work is essential in the ongoing battle between encryption and decryption, where each side seeks to outsmart the other in a constantly evolving digital landscape.

In the realm of modern cryptanalysis, tools and technologies have become indispensable for unraveling the secrets of encrypted data. Imagine these tools as the Sherlock Holmes of the digital world, helping cryptanalysts decipher the mysteries concealed within cryptographic algorithms and systems.

One of the fundamental tools for modern cryptanalysis is the use of powerful computers and high-performance computing clusters. Imagine harnessing the computational muscle of supercomputers to perform complex calculations and brute-force attacks on cryptographic keys. These machines can significantly expedite the cryptanalysis process, especially for encryption algorithms with longer key lengths.

Cryptanalysts often employ specialized software for their work. Imagine using custom-developed software to automate various cryptanalysis techniques. This software can range from tools that aid in analyzing ciphertext patterns to applications that simulate cryptographic attacks.

Cryptanalysis also relies on mathematical algorithms and libraries. Imagine leveraging mathematical algorithms to test the security of cryptographic systems. These algorithms help cryptanalysts probe the strengths and weaknesses of encryption algorithms and cryptographic protocols.

In the realm of side-channel attacks, specialized hardware and sensors are indispensable. Imagine using oscilloscopes to measure power consumption or electromagnetic radiation from a cryptographic device. These measurements provide valuable insights for side-channel attacks and can reveal sensitive information about the encryption process.

Quantum computers are on the horizon as both a threat and a tool for cryptanalysis. Imagine quantum computers as double-edged swords, capable of breaking traditional encryption methods but also helping cryptanalysts develop quantum-resistant encryption algorithms. Cryptanalysts must stay ahead by understanding quantum principles and their implications for cryptography.

Reverse engineering tools play a vital role in analyzing the inner workings of cryptographic software and hardware. Imagine dissecting cryptographic algorithms to understand their implementation details. These tools help cryptanalysts uncover vulnerabilities and weaknesses that can be exploited for attacks.

Rainbow tables and precomputed dictionaries are essential for attacking hashed passwords. Imagine these tables as vast databases containing precomputed hash values and their corresponding plaintexts. Cryptanalysts use rainbow tables to crack password hashes quickly and gain access to protected accounts.

Network analysis tools are crucial for cryptanalysts examining communication between devices and systems.

Imagine analyzing network traffic to identify patterns and vulnerabilities in cryptographic protocols. These tools enable cryptanalysts to discover weaknesses in the encryption of data transmitted over networks.

Hardware security modules (HSMs) are used to protect cryptographic keys and sensitive data. Imagine cryptanalysts attempting to breach the security of an HSM to access encrypted keys. These devices are formidable challenges, but their security can be compromised through various techniques.

The adoption of machine learning and artificial intelligence (AI) has opened new horizons in cryptanalysis. Imagine using machine learning algorithms to detect patterns in ciphertext or predict encryption keys. These AI-driven approaches can augment traditional cryptanalysis methods, making them more efficient and effective.

Cryptanalysts also rely on advanced statistical analysis tools. Imagine analyzing ciphertext using statistical techniques to identify patterns or weaknesses. These analyses can reveal information about encryption keys or the encryption algorithm itself.

In the context of post-quantum cryptography, researchers use quantum simulators. Imagine simulating the behavior of quantum computers to test the resilience of cryptographic algorithms. These simulators help cryptanalysts evaluate the security of encryption methods in a quantum-threatened world.

Collaborative platforms and open-source communities foster knowledge sharing among cryptanalysts. Imagine cryptanalysts from around the world collaborating on cryptographic challenges. These communities promote the exchange of ideas and insights, advancing the field of cryptanalysis.

Cryptanalysis is not solely a digital endeavor; physical access to cryptographic devices is often essential. Imagine cryptanalysts physically disassembling a secure hardware device to access its internal components. This approach allows them to manipulate the device and potentially extract encryption keys.

Cryptanalysts also make use of advanced mathematical modeling and simulation tools. Imagine creating mathematical models to represent cryptographic algorithms and systems. These models help cryptanalysts gain a deeper understanding of the encryption process and potential vulnerabilities.

In summary, tools and technologies are the cornerstone of modern cryptanalysis, enabling cryptanalysts to explore the intricacies of encryption algorithms and cryptographic systems. Imagine these tools as indispensable companions on the cryptanalyst's journey, aiding in the deciphering of encrypted data and the discovery of vulnerabilities. As technology continues to evolve, cryptanalysts will rely on increasingly sophisticated tools to navigate the complex landscape of cryptography and digital security.

Chapter 5: Differential and Linear Cryptanalysis

Differential cryptanalysis is a powerful technique used by cryptanalysts to analyze and break cryptographic systems. Imagine it as a detective's magnifying glass, revealing subtle differences in ciphertexts and uncovering hidden information about encryption keys.

At its core, differential cryptanalysis focuses on differences between pairs of plaintexts and the corresponding ciphertexts. Imagine taking two similar plaintexts and encrypting them using the same key; the goal is to find patterns in the differences between the resulting ciphertexts.

One of the fundamental principles of differential cryptanalysis is the concept of a "differential." Imagine a differential as a pair of plaintexts with a specific difference between them. For example, if we have two plaintexts, A and B, with a difference of D ($A \oplus B = D$), this constitutes a differential.

The cryptanalyst's objective is to analyze how this differential propagates through the encryption process. Imagine the encryption process as a series of mathematical operations, such as substitutions and permutations. The cryptanalyst observes how the differential evolves at each step.

Differential cryptanalysis often targets symmetric key ciphers, which use the same key for both encryption and decryption. Imagine an encryption algorithm where a key K is used to encrypt plaintexts and the same key K is used to decrypt ciphertexts. Differential cryptanalysis seeks to exploit the differences between plaintext pairs to recover the key K.

Let's delve deeper into the process of differential cryptanalysis. Imagine you have a pair of plaintexts, A and B, and you encrypt them to obtain ciphertexts C and D. You then calculate the difference between the ciphertexts, C $\oplus$ D, which represents the differential at the output of the encryption.

Cryptanalysts perform this process for multiple plaintext pairs, collecting a set of differentials. Imagine collecting a dataset of differentials that correspond to various plaintext differences and their corresponding ciphertext differences.

The cryptanalyst's task is to find a differential that exhibits a specific pattern or property. Imagine searching for a differential that results in a ciphertext difference that reveals information about the encryption key.

To achieve this, cryptanalysts use statistical analysis and mathematical techniques. Imagine employing statistical tools to identify differentials with higher probabilities of leading to key-related information. These probabilities are crucial in selecting the right differential for analysis.

Differential cryptanalysis often involves iteratively narrowing down the potential differentials. Imagine refining the search by eliminating less promising differentials and focusing on those that are more likely to yield results. This process requires a deep understanding of the encryption algorithm's internal workings.

A critical aspect of differential cryptanalysis is the concept of "differential characteristics." Imagine these as sequences of differentials that describe how a specific differential propagates through the encryption process.

These characteristics help cryptanalysts predict how the differential evolves.

Cryptanalysts work to construct differential characteristics that have high probabilities of revealing key information. Imagine crafting a roadmap of differentials that, when followed, can lead to the recovery of the encryption key.

Differential cryptanalysis is not limited to theoretical exercises; it has real-world applications. Imagine using differential cryptanalysis to break cryptographic systems in practice, such as recovering the keys used to secure sensitive data.

One of the earliest and most notable successes of differential cryptanalysis was breaking the Data Encryption Standard (DES) in the 1970s. Imagine the significance of this achievement; DES was a widely used encryption standard at the time.

In the DES cryptanalysis, the cryptanalysts constructed differential characteristics that revealed key information efficiently. Imagine the satisfaction of successfully recovering the secret keys and decrypting DES-encrypted data.

Since then, differential cryptanalysis has been applied to various encryption algorithms, both symmetric and asymmetric. Imagine cryptanalysts continually adapting and refining their techniques to tackle new cryptographic challenges.

Differential cryptanalysis remains a valuable tool in the cryptanalyst's toolkit. Imagine it as a versatile instrument, capable of dissecting and deciphering the inner workings of cryptographic systems.

It's essential to note that while differential cryptanalysis is a powerful technique, modern cryptographic algorithms are designed to resist such attacks. Imagine the ongoing cat-and-mouse game between cryptanalysts and cryptographic designers, where each seeks to outsmart the other.

In summary, differential cryptanalysis is a fascinating and powerful technique that revolves around the analysis of differences in plaintexts and ciphertexts. Imagine it as a methodical investigation into the behavior of cryptographic algorithms, with the goal of unveiling their secrets. Cryptanalysts leverage this technique to break cryptographic systems, and it has played a pivotal role in the history of cryptography. Linear cryptanalysis is another powerful technique in the arsenal of cryptanalysts, offering a different approach to breaking cryptographic systems. Imagine it as a method that seeks to find linear equations between the bits of plaintext, ciphertext, and the key used in encryption.

At its core, linear cryptanalysis focuses on identifying linear approximations of the cryptographic algorithm. Imagine it as a quest to uncover linear relationships between the input and output of the encryption process.

In linear cryptanalysis, cryptanalysts create linear equations that approximate the behavior of the encryption algorithm. Imagine these equations as mathematical representations of how the plaintext, ciphertext, and key bits interact.

The goal of linear cryptanalysis is to find linear equations with a high probability of holding true for a given encryption algorithm. Imagine these equations as clues that, when followed, can lead to the discovery of the encryption key.

One of the key challenges in linear cryptanalysis is the need for a large number of plaintext-ciphertext pairs. Imagine the cryptanalyst collecting a vast dataset of these pairs to perform the analysis effectively.

Each plaintext-ciphertext pair contributes to the creation of linear equations. Imagine these pairs as pieces of a puzzle, with each piece providing a bit of insight into the behavior of the encryption algorithm.

Cryptanalysts employ statistical tools to assess the strength of linear approximations. Imagine these tools as a means to evaluate which linear equations are likely to reveal key-related information.

Linear cryptanalysis is often used against block ciphers, where the encryption algorithm processes data in fixed-size blocks. Imagine it as a technique tailored to the specific structure of block ciphers.

The cryptanalyst's journey begins with the selection of a specific part of the encryption algorithm to analyze. Imagine this as choosing a starting point in the algorithm's intricate maze.

Once a starting point is chosen, cryptanalysts create linear equations that describe how changes in the plaintext and key affect changes in the ciphertext. Imagine these equations as the cryptanalyst's map through the maze.

The success of linear cryptanalysis relies on the cryptanalyst's ability to construct linear equations that hold true with high probability. Imagine this process as akin to finding the right path through a labyrinth.

Cryptanalysts often use computer simulations to test the strength of their linear approximations. Imagine these simulations as a way to validate their hypotheses and fine-tune their linear equations.

Linear cryptanalysis is not limited to theoretical exercises; it has been applied successfully to real-world cryptographic systems. Imagine cryptanalysts leveraging this technique to recover encryption keys protecting sensitive information.

One famous application of linear cryptanalysis was its use in breaking the Khufu and Khafre block ciphers. Imagine the excitement of cryptanalysts when they successfully deciphered encrypted messages using this technique.

Linear cryptanalysis continues to be a valuable tool in cryptanalysis, complementing other methods like differential cryptanalysis. Imagine it as one of the versatile instruments in the cryptanalyst's toolkit. It's important to note that the effectiveness of linear cryptanalysis depends on the specific encryption algorithm being analyzed. Imagine different algorithms as unique puzzles, each requiring a tailored approach. Modern cryptographic algorithms are designed with robustness against linear cryptanalysis in mind. Imagine this as a testament to the ongoing evolution of cryptography.

Cryptanalysis, including linear cryptanalysis, plays a critical role in the security of cryptographic systems. Imagine it as a constant battle between those who seek to protect information and those who aim to uncover its secrets.

In summary, linear cryptanalysis is a fascinating technique that seeks to uncover linear relationships within cryptographic algorithms. Imagine it as a methodical exploration of these algorithms, with the aim of revealing their inner workings. Cryptanalysts use this technique to break encryption and have achieved notable successes in the field.

Chapter 6: Cryptanalysis of Block Ciphers

Analyzing the security of block ciphers is a crucial endeavor in the field of cryptography. Imagine it as a thorough examination of the strength and resilience of these encryption algorithms.

Block ciphers are cryptographic algorithms that process data in fixed-size blocks, typically 64 or 128 bits. Imagine these blocks as individual chunks of data that the algorithm encrypts or decrypts.

One of the primary goals in analyzing block ciphers is to assess their resistance against attacks. Imagine these attacks as various strategies employed by adversaries to compromise the security of the cipher.

Security analysis often begins with evaluating the algorithm's resistance to known attacks. Imagine these known attacks as techniques that cryptanalysts have developed over time, such as differential and linear cryptanalysis.

Cryptanalysts use a variety of tools and techniques to evaluate the strength of block ciphers. Imagine these tools as instruments that help assess the algorithm's vulnerabilities.

One critical aspect of security analysis is understanding the algorithm's key space. Imagine the key space as the total number of possible keys that the cipher can use for encryption.

A larger key space means more possible keys, making it exponentially more challenging for an attacker to perform a brute-force attack. Imagine this as a vast maze where finding the correct key is like finding a needle in a haystack.

Statistical analysis is a fundamental part of security assessment. Imagine it as analyzing the patterns and distributions of ciphertexts and keys to detect any anomalies or weaknesses.

Another critical element is evaluating the diffusion and confusion properties of the block cipher. Imagine diffusion as the spreading of changes in the plaintext throughout the ciphertext.

Confusion, on the other hand, refers to the complexity of the relationship between the plaintext, the ciphertext, and the encryption key. Imagine it as making the relationship between them as intricate as possible.

Cryptanalysts also examine the algorithm's resistance to differential and linear cryptanalysis. Imagine these as probing techniques used to exploit any linear or differential relationships within the cipher.

The Avalanche Effect is a key concept in assessing a block cipher's security. Imagine it as the property where a small change in the input (plaintext or key) leads to a significant change in the output (ciphertext).

A block cipher is considered secure if it exhibits a strong Avalanche Effect, making it challenging for attackers to predict the output given slight changes in the input.

Security analysis also involves studying the algorithm's S-boxes, which are nonlinear components that introduce confusion. Imagine them as intricate puzzles that adversaries must solve to break the cipher.

The resistance of block ciphers against side-channel attacks is another crucial consideration. Imagine these attacks as attempts to gather information about the encryption process from physical characteristics like power consumption or timing.

Cryptanalysts often employ mathematical models to simulate attacks on block ciphers. Imagine these models as virtual testing environments where potential vulnerabilities are explored.

One famous example of a secure block cipher is the Advanced Encryption Standard (AES). Imagine AES as a robust fortress in the world of cryptography, known for its resilience against attacks.

AES underwent extensive security analysis before being adopted as a standard. Imagine this analysis as a rigorous series of tests and evaluations to ensure its strength.

In recent years, the development of lightweight block ciphers has gained prominence. Imagine these ciphers as designed for resource-constrained environments like IoT devices, where efficiency and security are paramount.

Analyzing the security of lightweight block ciphers presents unique challenges and requires innovative approaches. Imagine it as adapting to new frontiers in the ever-evolving field of cryptography.

The security of block ciphers is not static; it evolves with advancements in cryptanalysis and computing power. Imagine it as a constant race between those who build strong ciphers and those who attempt to break them.

In summary, analyzing the security of block ciphers is a critical task in ensuring the protection of sensitive information. Imagine it as a continuous journey of evaluating and fortifying encryption algorithms against the ever-present threat of attacks. Cryptanalysts play a vital role in this ongoing battle, striving to keep cryptographic systems secure in an increasingly digital world.

Block ciphers are fundamental components of modern cryptography, serving as the building blocks for secure communication and data protection. As technology advances, so do the techniques employed by cryptanalysts to analyze and potentially break these ciphers. Imagine block cipher cryptanalysis as a high-stakes chess game, with cryptanalysts strategizing to uncover vulnerabilities while cipher designers work diligently to fortify their creations.

Advanced techniques for block cipher cryptanalysis delve into the intricate details of these encryption algorithms, aiming to identify weaknesses that might be exploited by adversaries. This journey begins with a deep understanding of the cipher's inner workings, its mathematical foundations, and the various components that make it resistant to attacks.

One notable technique in block cipher cryptanalysis is differential cryptanalysis, which focuses on how changes in the plaintext and key impact changes in the ciphertext. Imagine this technique as a detective's keen eye, searching for subtle patterns and correlations that can reveal the encryption key.

Differential cryptanalysis involves crafting pairs of plaintexts and ciphertexts with specific differences and then analyzing how these differences propagate through the encryption process. This propagation of differences serves as a breadcrumb trail that cryptanalysts follow, inching closer to the secret key.

To successfully employ differential cryptanalysis, cryptanalysts must collect a considerable number of plaintext-ciphertext pairs. Imagine these pairs as pieces of evidence, with each pair providing a glimpse into the cipher's behavior. The more evidence gathered, the more refined the analysis becomes.

Statistical tools play a crucial role in the cryptanalyst's toolkit when conducting differential cryptanalysis. These tools allow cryptanalysts to assess the significance of observed differences and determine the likelihood of recovering the encryption key. Think of these tools as magnifying glasses that help reveal hidden patterns.

Another powerful technique in block cipher cryptanalysis is linear cryptanalysis. While differential cryptanalysis focuses on differences, linear cryptanalysis explores linear approximations of the cipher's behavior. Imagine it as constructing equations that represent the relationships between plaintext, ciphertext, and key bits in a linear fashion.

Linear cryptanalysis seeks equations with a high probability of holding true for a given cipher. These equations serve as clues that, when pieced together, can unveil the encryption key. Imagine solving a complex puzzle by assembling the right pieces, and each equation is a piece of the cryptographic puzzle.

Successful linear cryptanalysis often requires a significant amount of computational power and mathematical expertise. Cryptanalysts leverage computational tools to evaluate the strength of linear approximations and refine their analysis. Think of these tools as powerful allies in the quest to break the cipher.

Block cipher designers continually strive to thwart cryptanalysts' efforts by creating ciphers with robust resistance to these techniques. This dynamic cat-and-mouse game between cryptanalysts and cipher designers fuels innovation on both sides. Imagine it as a constant push for excellence in cryptography.

In addition to differential and linear cryptanalysis, advanced cryptanalysts explore various other techniques tailored to specific cipher structures and weaknesses. These techniques range from algebraic attacks to integral attacks, each offering a unique perspective on the cipher's vulnerabilities.

Algebraic attacks, for example, leverage algebraic structures within the cipher to deduce key information. Imagine this technique as deciphering a cryptic code by solving algebraic equations embedded within the cipher's mathematical framework.

Integral attacks focus on the cumulative effect of differences across multiple rounds of the cipher. Imagine it as observing how small ripples in a pond can combine to create larger waves, ultimately revealing the key's location.

The success of block cipher cryptanalysis hinges on the cryptanalyst's ability to adapt and innovate. Each cipher presents its own set of challenges and opportunities, and cryptanalysts must tailor their techniques accordingly. This adaptability is akin to a versatile toolset, with each tool designed for a specific task.

One essential aspect of advanced block cipher cryptanalysis is collaboration and information sharing within the cryptography community. Cryptanalysts often work together to pool their expertise and insights, collectively advancing the field. Imagine it as a global network of puzzle solvers, collaborating to crack the most complex ciphers.

As technology continues to evolve, the arms race between cipher designers and cryptanalysts persists. The security of block ciphers remains paramount, as they safeguard sensitive information in various applications, from secure communications to financial transactions.

In summary, advanced techniques for block cipher cryptanalysis represent the forefront of cryptographic research and analysis. Cryptanalysts employ a diverse array of methods, from differential and linear cryptanalysis to algebraic and integral attacks, in their pursuit of uncovering vulnerabilities within encryption algorithms. This ongoing quest for security and resilience in the face of ever-advancing technology defines the dynamic landscape of modern cryptography.

Chapter 7: Cryptanalysis of Stream Ciphers

Stream ciphers are cryptographic algorithms that operate on individual bits or bytes of data, making them distinct from block ciphers. In the world of cryptography, they serve as essential tools for secure communication and data protection, just like their block cipher counterparts. However, like any cryptographic system, stream ciphers are subject to analysis and potential vulnerabilities that cryptanalysts strive to uncover.

Stream cipher cryptanalysis methods are a diverse set of techniques and strategies designed to scrutinize these ciphers, searching for weaknesses that could be exploited by malicious actors. Imagine cryptanalysis as a detective's quest for clues, with each technique revealing a piece of the puzzle that leads to the encryption key.

One fundamental approach in stream cipher cryptanalysis is known as keystream recovery. The keystream is the sequence of random or pseudorandom bits generated by the cipher and combined with the plaintext to produce the ciphertext. Imagine this keystream as the ink used in a cryptographic pen, and the goal of cryptanalysts is to reverse-engineer this ink to reveal the original message.

Keystream recovery typically involves collecting a significant amount of known plaintext and corresponding ciphertext. This known plaintext serves as the starting point for cryptanalysts, as it provides a basis for comparing the ciphertext with the predicted keystream. Think of it as matching pieces of a jigsaw puzzle, with each known plaintext-ciphertext pair helping to reconstruct the keystream.

To recover the keystream successfully, cryptanalysts often employ statistical analysis and computational techniques. These tools allow them to identify patterns or biases in the keystream generation process. Imagine statistical analysis as a magnifying glass that reveals subtle irregularities in the ink's texture, aiding in its reconstruction.

A well-known keystream recovery technique for stream ciphers is the correlation attack. This attack exploits correlations between the keystream bits and the ciphertext bits. Imagine it as studying the behavior of ink drops on a canvas, where the position and shape of one drop can provide insights into others nearby.

The correlation attack seeks to find linear relationships between the keystream bits and the ciphertext bits. These relationships are akin to discovering how the ink drops interact on the canvas, allowing cryptanalysts to predict the keystream more accurately. The success of this attack depends on the cipher's design and the quality of the keystream generation.

Another important aspect of stream cipher cryptanalysis is the examination of the cipher's internal structure. Stream ciphers are often built on mathematical algorithms, and understanding these algorithms is crucial for cryptanalysts. Imagine it as deciphering the blueprint of a complex machine; once you understand how it works, you can identify its vulnerabilities.

One common target in the analysis of stream cipher internals is the feedback mechanism. Stream ciphers frequently employ feedback to generate the keystream, and cryptanalysts scrutinize this process for weaknesses.

Think of it as inspecting the gears and levers of a machine to identify any loose or faulty components.

Cryptanalysts may also explore the cipher's key schedule, which determines how the encryption key is used to generate the keystream. Understanding the key schedule is akin to deciphering the machine's control panel; it allows cryptanalysts to manipulate the process to their advantage.

In addition to keystream recovery and internal structure analysis, cryptanalysts may explore other avenues, such as algebraic attacks and correlation-based techniques. Algebraic attacks focus on modeling the cipher's behavior using algebraic equations, providing a systematic approach to keystream recovery.

Correlation-based techniques, on the other hand, examine the relationships between different portions of the keystream and ciphertext. These techniques are akin to studying how different colors blend on an artist's palette, seeking patterns that reveal the encryption key.

Successful stream cipher cryptanalysis often requires a combination of these techniques, as well as a deep understanding of the cipher's design and mathematical underpinnings. It's a dynamic and evolving field where cryptanalysts continually adapt to the latest developments in cryptography.

Collaboration and information sharing within the cryptography community are essential for advancing stream cipher cryptanalysis. Cryptanalysts often work together to exchange insights and discoveries, collectively improving their understanding of stream ciphers and enhancing security.

In summary, stream cipher cryptanalysis methods are an integral part of the broader field of cryptography. They involve a diverse set of techniques aimed at uncovering vulnerabilities in stream ciphers, ultimately contributing to the ongoing quest for secure communication and data protection. Cryptanalysts play a vital role in this endeavor, employing their expertise and innovation to strengthen the foundations of cryptographic security.

In the realm of cryptography, stream ciphers serve as indispensable tools for encrypting data, ensuring its confidentiality and security during transmission. These ciphers operate by generating a keystream, a sequence of pseudorandom or random bits, which is then combined with the plaintext to produce the ciphertext. While stream ciphers are widely used and can provide robust security when properly designed and implemented, they are not immune to weaknesses and vulnerabilities that cryptanalysts diligently seek to exploit.

One of the primary vulnerabilities in stream ciphers is related to the keystream generation process. The keystream should ideally exhibit the properties of randomness, making it indistinguishable from truly random data. However, any deviation from true randomness can introduce predictability and compromise security. Think of it as trying to mimic the seemingly chaotic pattern of rainfall on a window; any discernible regularity would make the process less secure.

One vulnerability in keystream generation is the potential for bias or correlation between keystream bits. If cryptanalysts detect patterns or correlations in the keystream, they can leverage this information to predict subsequent bits. Imagine it as discovering that raindrops tend to fall in certain patterns rather than randomly; this predictability can be exploited to compromise the security of the cipher.

To mitigate this vulnerability, stream ciphers use pseudorandom number generators (PRNGs) or random number generators (RNGs) to produce keystreams. PRNGs are mathematical algorithms designed to generate sequences that appear random, while RNGs rely on unpredictable physical processes, such as electronic noise. These generators are carefully designed and tested to minimize biases and correlations, but vulnerabilities can still emerge if the design or implementation is flawed.

Another vulnerability in stream ciphers lies in the key management and distribution process. Like all cryptographic systems, the security of a stream cipher depends on the secrecy and integrity of the encryption key. If an adversary gains access to the key, they can decrypt the ciphertext and compromise the data's confidentiality. Think of the key as the key to a locked safe; if someone obtains it, they can access the contents inside.

Key management involves generating, distributing, and storing encryption keys securely. Weaknesses in any of these stages can lead to key compromise. For example, if a key is generated using a predictable algorithm or is transmitted over an insecure channel, it becomes susceptible to interception and compromise. Imagine if a safe's combination was easily guessable or if the key to a treasure chest were left lying around unprotected.

To address key management vulnerabilities, cryptographic protocols and best practices are established to ensure the secure generation, distribution, and storage of encryption keys. These measures include using strong cryptographic algorithms for key generation, implementing secure key exchange protocols, and safeguarding keys through encryption and access controls.

Cryptanalysis techniques, as mentioned earlier, also play a crucial role in uncovering vulnerabilities in stream ciphers. Cryptanalysts diligently analyze ciphertexts to discern patterns, biases, or correlations that could lead to keystream recovery. They leverage statistical analysis, mathematical modeling, and computational power to mount attacks on stream ciphers. Think of them as skilled detectives examining clues to unlock the secrets concealed within the ciphertext.

One well-known vulnerability in stream ciphers is the potential for a ciphertext-only attack. In such an attack scenario, the cryptanalyst has access only to the ciphertext and no knowledge of the plaintext or the key. Despite these limitations, cryptanalysts have developed sophisticated techniques, such as frequency analysis and correlation attacks, to infer information about the keystream and potentially recover the encryption key.

Frequency analysis involves examining the distribution of ciphertext symbols, such as letters or bits, to identify patterns that may correspond to the plaintext or the keystream. Imagine analyzing the frequency of letters in a coded message to deduce the language being used; this can provide valuable insights into the ciphertext.

Correlation attacks, on the other hand, exploit statistical relationships between the ciphertext and the keystream to deduce information about the key. These attacks seek to uncover correlations that can be leveraged to predict parts of the keystream, ultimately leading to key recovery. Think of it as deducing the code for a locked door by observing how it responds to different keys.

Stream cipher vulnerabilities can also stem from implementation flaws rather than weaknesses in the underlying algorithm. Poorly implemented stream ciphers may inadvertently introduce biases or patterns into the keystream, making it more predictable and vulnerable to attack. Think of it as building a lock with a flaw that makes it easier to pick.

To mitigate implementation vulnerabilities, rigorous testing and validation processes are crucial. Cryptographers and security experts perform extensive audits and assessments of cryptographic implementations to identify and rectify potential flaws. Secure coding practices and regular updates are essential to maintaining the resilience of stream ciphers.

In summary, while stream ciphers are powerful tools for data encryption, they are not immune to vulnerabilities and weaknesses. The generation of a secure keystream, robust key management, and resilient implementation are essential factors in mitigating these vulnerabilities. Cryptanalysts continue to push the boundaries of cryptographic security, uncovering weaknesses and driving innovation in the field to ensure the ongoing protection of sensitive data.

Chapter 8: Attacks on Public Key Cryptosystems

In the world of cryptography, the security of public key cryptosystems is of paramount importance, as they underpin the security of digital communication and data protection in the digital age. Public key cryptosystems are designed to offer robust security by using two distinct keys, a public key for encryption and a private key for decryption. While these systems have proven effective at safeguarding data, they are not immune to cryptanalysis, a field of study dedicated to analyzing and potentially breaking cryptographic systems.

Cryptanalysis against public key cryptosystems presents a unique set of challenges and opportunities for cryptanalysts. Unlike symmetric key cryptosystems, where the same key is used for both encryption and decryption, public key cryptosystems rely on the mathematical relationship between a public key and a private key. This relationship is typically based on mathematical problems that are considered hard to solve, such as integer factorization or the discrete logarithm problem.

One of the most well-known public key cryptosystems is the RSA encryption algorithm, which is based on the difficulty of factoring the product of two large prime numbers. RSA encryption has been widely used for securing data transmission over the internet, but it is not without its vulnerabilities, especially when improperly configured or when weak key lengths are used.

Cryptanalysts have developed various approaches to attack RSA encryption, with one of the most prominent being the factorization of the modulus, known as the RSA factorization problem. The RSA factorization problem involves finding the two prime factors of a large composite number, which forms the basis of the RSA public key. If an attacker can successfully factor the modulus, they can compute the private key and decrypt the encrypted data.

To address this vulnerability, cryptographers have recommended the use of larger key sizes to increase the difficulty of factorization. While a 2048-bit or 3072-bit RSA key is currently considered secure, advances in computational power and cryptanalysis techniques may necessitate even larger key sizes in the future.

Another approach to cryptanalysis against RSA is the consideration of side-channel attacks. Side-channel attacks exploit unintended information leakage from cryptographic devices, such as timing information, power consumption, or electromagnetic radiation. By analyzing these side-channel signals, attackers can gain insights into the internal operations of the cryptosystem and potentially recover the private key.

To defend against side-channel attacks, cryptographers have developed countermeasures, including the use of constant-time algorithms and hardware protections. These measures aim to eliminate or minimize the leakage of sensitive information during cryptographic operations.

In addition to RSA, another widely used public key cryptosystem is the Diffie-Hellman key exchange protocol, which forms the basis for secure key exchange in many communication protocols, including SSL/TLS for secure web browsing. The security of Diffie-Hellman relies on the discrete logarithm problem, which involves finding the exponent of a given number in a finite field.

Cryptanalysis against Diffie-Hellman often involves attempts to compute discrete logarithms in the underlying finite field. Various algorithms, such as Pollard's rho algorithm and the index calculus method, have been developed to solve the discrete logarithm problem efficiently. The security of Diffie-Hellman depends on the choice of parameters and the size of the finite field, with larger field sizes providing greater resistance to cryptanalysis.

A significant development in recent years has been the emergence of quantum computing as a potential threat to public key cryptosystems. Quantum computers have the potential to solve certain mathematical problems, including integer factorization and discrete logarithms, much more efficiently than classical computers. Shor's algorithm, for example, can factor large numbers in polynomial time on a quantum computer, posing a significant threat to RSA encryption and other cryptosystems based on similar problems.

To counter the threat of quantum computing, the field of post-quantum cryptography has emerged. Post-quantum cryptographic algorithms are designed to resist attacks by quantum computers. These algorithms are being actively researched and standardized to ensure the long-term security of digital communication.

In the realm of elliptic curve cryptography (ECC), which is another widely used public key cryptosystem, cryptanalysis efforts focus on the elliptic curve discrete logarithm problem (ECDLP). The security of ECC depends on the difficulty of finding the discrete logarithm of a point on an elliptic curve.

Efforts to cryptanalyze ECC often involve advances in algorithms for solving the ECDLP, as well as improvements in computational methods. One well-known algorithm for solving the ECDLP is Pollard's rho algorithm, which aims to find the discrete logarithm by searching for collisions in the group generated by the elliptic curve point.

To enhance the security of ECC, elliptic curves with specific properties, such as those with large prime orders and carefully chosen parameters, are recommended. Additionally, the use of ECC with larger key sizes can further increase security.

In the realm of public key infrastructure (PKI), which is essential for secure communication and digital identity verification, cryptanalysis efforts may target weaknesses in certificate issuance and management processes. Attackers may attempt to compromise certificate authorities (CAs) or intercept certificate requests to impersonate legitimate entities.

To mitigate these risks, PKI practitioners implement stringent security measures, including rigorous vetting of CAs, certificate revocation mechanisms, and the use of certificate transparency logs. These measures aim to maintain the integrity and trustworthiness of the PKI ecosystem.

Cryptanalysis against public key cryptosystems is an ongoing and evolving field, as both attackers and defenders continually adapt and innovate. Cryptographers and security experts work tirelessly to develop and evaluate new cryptographic algorithms and protocols to withstand emerging threats. The dynamic nature of the field ensures that public key cryptosystems remain a robust foundation for secure digital communication in an ever-changing landscape of threats and challenges.

In the realm of cybersecurity, understanding and addressing vulnerabilities in public key cryptography is essential for maintaining the integrity and security of digital communication. Public key cryptography, which relies on the mathematical relationship between a public key and a private key, forms the foundation of secure data transmission, digital signatures, and secure key exchange. However, no system is entirely immune to vulnerabilities, and cryptanalysts and malicious actors continually seek to exploit weaknesses in these cryptographic systems.

One of the most well-known vulnerabilities in public key cryptography is the factorization of large composite numbers, which underpins the RSA encryption algorithm. RSA encryption is widely used for securing data transmission over the internet, but its security relies on the presumed difficulty of factoring the product of two large prime numbers. If an attacker can successfully factor the modulus, they can compute the private key and decrypt the encrypted data.

To defend against factorization attacks, security experts recommend the use of sufficiently large key sizes. While a 2048-bit or 3072-bit RSA key is currently considered secure, advances in computational power and cryptanalysis techniques may necessitate even larger key sizes in the future.

Another vulnerability in public key cryptography pertains to the discrete logarithm problem, which forms the basis of cryptographic systems like the Diffie-Hellman key exchange protocol. The discrete logarithm problem involves finding the exponent of a given number in a finite field. Cryptanalysis efforts often involve attempts to compute discrete logarithms efficiently in the underlying finite field.

Various algorithms, such as Pollard's rho algorithm and the index calculus method, have been developed to solve the discrete logarithm problem efficiently. The security of Diffie-Hellman and similar systems depends on the choice of parameters and the size of the finite field, with larger field sizes providing greater resistance to cryptanalysis.

In the realm of elliptic curve cryptography (ECC), another widely used public key cryptosystem, vulnerabilities can arise from weaknesses in the elliptic curve discrete logarithm problem (ECDLP). The security of ECC depends on the presumed difficulty of finding the discrete logarithm of a point on an elliptic curve.

Efforts to exploit vulnerabilities in ECC often involve advances in algorithms for solving the ECDLP, as well as improvements in computational methods. Pollard's rho algorithm, for example, aims to find the discrete logarithm by searching for collisions in the group generated by the elliptic curve point.

To mitigate vulnerabilities in ECC, practitioners recommend the use of elliptic curves with specific properties, such as those with large prime orders and carefully chosen parameters. Additionally, the use of ECC with larger key sizes can further enhance security.

Beyond the realm of specific cryptographic algorithms, vulnerabilities in public key cryptography can also manifest in the broader public key infrastructure (PKI), which is crucial for secure communication and digital identity verification. Vulnerabilities in PKI can result from weaknesses in certificate issuance and management processes.

Attackers may attempt to compromise certificate authorities (CAs) or intercept certificate requests to impersonate legitimate entities. Such vulnerabilities can lead to fraudulent certificates being issued, undermining the trust and security of digital communication.

To mitigate these risks, stringent security measures are implemented within PKI ecosystems. These measures include thorough vetting of CAs, robust certificate revocation mechanisms, and the use of certificate transparency logs. These efforts aim to maintain the integrity and trustworthiness of the PKI ecosystem.

One notable development in recent years is the emergence of quantum computing as a potential threat to public key cryptography. Quantum computers have the potential to solve certain mathematical problems, including integer factorization and discrete logarithms, much more efficiently than classical computers.

Shor's algorithm, for example, can factor large numbers in polynomial time on a quantum computer, posing a significant threat to RSA encryption and other cryptosystems based on similar problems. To counter this threat, the field of post-quantum cryptography has emerged, with researchers actively working on cryptographic algorithms that resist attacks by quantum computers.

Vulnerabilities in public key cryptography are not limited to mathematical weaknesses alone. Cryptanalysts may also explore side-channel attacks, which exploit unintended information leakage from cryptographic devices. This leakage can include timing information, power consumption, or electromagnetic radiation.

By analyzing these side-channel signals, attackers can gain insights into the internal operations of the cryptosystem and potentially recover sensitive information, such as private keys. Countermeasures against side-channel attacks involve implementing constant-time algorithms, hardware protections, and secure key storage mechanisms.

In the evolving landscape of cybersecurity, understanding and addressing vulnerabilities in public key cryptography is an ongoing challenge. Cryptanalysts continually probe cryptographic systems for weaknesses, while security experts work tirelessly to develop and evaluate new cryptographic algorithms and protocols to withstand emerging threats.

The dynamic nature of this field ensures that vulnerabilities are identified and mitigated to maintain the security and integrity of digital communication and data protection in an ever-changing landscape of challenges and risks.

Chapter 9: Quantum Cryptanalysis

Quantum algorithms for cryptanalysis represent a significant paradigm shift in the world of cryptography, with the potential to disrupt the security of many widely used encryption schemes. Traditional cryptographic systems rely on the perceived computational difficulty of certain mathematical problems, such as factoring large numbers or computing discrete logarithms. Quantum computers, however, have the capability to solve these problems exponentially faster than classical computers using quantum algorithms.

One of the most famous quantum algorithms that poses a significant threat to classical encryption is Shor's algorithm. Shor's algorithm, devised by mathematician Peter Shor in 1994, is designed to efficiently factor large numbers. This poses a substantial challenge to widely used encryption methods like RSA, which depend on the difficulty of factoring the product of two large prime numbers.

The classical factoring problem, which forms the basis of RSA encryption, becomes trivial for a sufficiently powerful quantum computer running Shor's algorithm. It is worth noting that, while quantum computers capable of executing Shor's algorithm do not yet exist, the theoretical groundwork has been laid, and researchers are actively working on developing practical quantum computing technology.

Another quantum algorithm with profound implications for cryptography is Grover's algorithm. Proposed by Lov Grover in 1996, this algorithm is designed to perform unstructured search quadratically faster than classical algorithms. Grover's algorithm can be employed to break symmetric key encryption by searching through all possible keys to find the correct one.

While Grover's algorithm does not provide the exponential speedup seen in Shor's algorithm, it still has the potential to halve the effective key length of symmetric ciphers. For example, a 128-bit AES key, which is considered secure against classical brute-force attacks, would offer the same level of security as a 64-bit key when subjected to Grover's algorithm.

The advent of quantum computing also raises concerns about the security of widely used cryptographic protocols like the Diffie-Hellman key exchange. The Diffie-Hellman protocol, which relies on the difficulty of computing discrete logarithms in finite fields, becomes vulnerable to quantum attacks with the emergence of large-scale quantum computers.

Quantum computers have the potential to efficiently compute discrete logarithms, which could allow attackers to compromise the confidentiality of encrypted communications established using the Diffie-Hellman key exchange. This has led to the development of post-quantum cryptographic alternatives that aim to resist quantum attacks.

Post-quantum cryptography encompasses a broad range of cryptographic schemes and algorithms that are specifically designed to be secure against quantum attacks. These alternatives often rely on different mathematical problems that are believed to be difficult for quantum computers to solve efficiently.

One approach in post-quantum cryptography is lattice-based cryptography, which builds cryptographic systems on the hardness of lattice problems. Lattice problems involve finding the shortest vector in a lattice, and they are believed to be difficult for both classical and quantum computers to solve efficiently.

Another promising avenue is code-based cryptography, which relies on the hardness of decoding randomly generated linear codes. Code-based encryption schemes are resistant to Shor's algorithm and are considered a strong candidate for post-quantum security.

Multivariate polynomial cryptography is yet another post-quantum approach that hinges on the difficulty of solving systems of multivariate polynomial equations. These systems are designed to be resistant to quantum attacks by increasing the complexity of solving the underlying mathematical problems.

Furthermore, hash-based cryptography is an area of interest in post-quantum security. Hash-based digital signatures and Merkle tree-based structures offer robust security against quantum attacks. These cryptographic primitives have the advantage of being well-understood and having a long history of use in various applications.

While the threat of quantum computers to classical encryption algorithms is significant, it is important to note that the timeline for the development of practical quantum computers capable of executing Shor's and Grover's algorithms remains uncertain. Researchers, organizations, and governments are actively investing in quantum-resistant cryptography to ensure the security of digital communication in a post-quantum era.

In summary, quantum algorithms for cryptanalysis represent a groundbreaking challenge to classical encryption methods. Shor's algorithm and Grover's algorithm have the potential to significantly reduce the security of widely used encryption schemes. However, the field of post-quantum cryptography is actively exploring alternative cryptographic approaches that are resistant to quantum attacks. While the timeline for the emergence of practical quantum computers remains uncertain, the importance of developing and adopting quantum-resistant cryptographic solutions cannot be overstated in ensuring the long-term security of digital communication and data protection. Quantum computing has emerged as a revolutionary field of study with the potential to reshape the landscape of cryptography and information security in profound ways. The unique capabilities of quantum computers have raised concerns and challenges for the security of traditional cryptographic systems that have long been the foundation of secure digital communication. At the heart of the quantum computing revolution lies the fundamental difference between classical and quantum computing principles. Classical computers process data in binary bits, which can exist in one of two states: 0 or 1. Quantum computers, on the other hand, use quantum bits or qubits, which can exist in a superposition of states. This allows quantum computers to perform certain calculations exponentially faster than their classical counterparts.

One of the most widely recognized quantum algorithms with implications for cryptography is Shor's algorithm, which was developed by Peter Shor in 1994. Shor's algorithm is designed to efficiently factor large numbers, a task that is classically believed to be computationally difficult. Factoring large numbers is at the core of several widely used encryption schemes, including RSA.

In RSA encryption, the security of the system relies on the fact that factoring a large composite number into its prime factors is a time-consuming process for classical computers. However, Shor's algorithm has the potential to factor large numbers exponentially faster on a sufficiently powerful quantum computer, posing a significant threat to RSA encryption.

The impact of Shor's algorithm on RSA encryption has prompted the cryptography community to explore alternative post-quantum cryptographic solutions that are resistant to quantum attacks. These solutions aim to replace or supplement existing cryptographic algorithms with methods that remain secure even in the face of quantum computers.

Another quantum algorithm of great concern for cryptographic systems is Grover's algorithm, developed by Lov Grover in 1996. Grover's algorithm is designed for unstructured search, and it can search through an unsorted database of N items in $O(\sqrt{N})$ time, providing a quadratic speedup over classical search algorithms.

In the context of cryptography, Grover's algorithm raises concerns for symmetric key encryption. Symmetric key encryption relies on the security of a secret key that needs to be kept secret from potential attackers. Classical brute-force attacks against symmetric encryption involve trying all possible keys, which takes exponential time. However, Grover's algorithm can effectively halve the search space for symmetric keys, making it twice as fast as classical brute-force attacks.

To maintain the same level of security against Grover's algorithm as against classical attacks, the key length for symmetric encryption schemes must be doubled. For example, a 128-bit AES key, which is considered secure against classical brute-force attacks, would need to be increased to a 256-bit key to maintain security against Grover's algorithm.

Furthermore, quantum computing poses a threat to other widely used cryptographic protocols, such as the Diffie-Hellman key exchange. The security of Diffie-Hellman relies on the difficulty of solving discrete logarithm problems in finite fields. Quantum computers have the potential to efficiently compute discrete logarithms, which could compromise the confidentiality of encrypted communications established using this protocol.

The advent of quantum computing has spurred intense research and development efforts in the field of post-quantum cryptography. Post-quantum cryptography encompasses a variety of cryptographic approaches and algorithms that are designed to resist quantum attacks. These approaches often rely on mathematical problems that are believed to be hard even for quantum computers.

One notable approach is lattice-based cryptography, which builds cryptographic systems on the hardness of lattice problems. Lattice problems involve finding the shortest vector in a lattice, and they are considered difficult for both classical and quantum computers.

Code-based cryptography is another promising avenue in post-quantum cryptography. It relies on the difficulty of decoding randomly generated linear codes. Code-based encryption schemes are resistant to Shor's algorithm and are considered strong candidates for post-quantum security.

Multivariate polynomial cryptography is yet another post-quantum approach that hinges on the difficulty of solving systems of multivariate polynomial equations. These systems are designed to be resistant to quantum attacks by increasing the complexity of solving the underlying mathematical problems.

Additionally, hash-based cryptography is an area of interest in post-quantum security. Hash-based digital signatures and Merkle tree-based structures offer robust security against quantum attacks. These cryptographic primitives are well-understood and have a long history of use in various applications.

The development and adoption of post-quantum cryptographic solutions are critical to ensuring the long-term security of digital communication and data protection in a world where quantum computers may become a reality. Organizations and governments around the world are actively investing in research and the standardization of post-quantum cryptographic algorithms to prepare for the post-quantum era.

In summary, quantum computing has the potential to disrupt the security of traditional cryptographic systems, and the development of quantum-resistant cryptography is of paramount importance. Shor's and Grover's algorithms, among others, pose significant threats to classical encryption methods, leading to the exploration of alternative cryptographic solutions that can withstand quantum attacks. As quantum computing technology advances, the field of post-quantum cryptography will continue to evolve to meet the challenges of an increasingly quantum-enabled world.

Chapter 10: Countermeasures and Defense Strategies

As we delve deeper into the world of cryptography and information security, it becomes increasingly evident that the landscape is ever-evolving, and so are the threats that attempt to breach its defenses. In response to these challenges, cryptographic countermeasures play a pivotal role in safeguarding our data and communication channels from malicious actors.

One fundamental aspect of cryptographic countermeasures is the concept of defense in depth. This approach emphasizes layering multiple security measures to protect against a variety of attacks, making it difficult for adversaries to compromise a system. Just as a castle in medieval times had outer walls, moats, and inner fortifications, modern cryptographic systems are fortified with multiple layers of protection.

One of the essential countermeasures is key management. Properly managing cryptographic keys is fundamental to the security of any cryptographic system. Encryption keys should be generated securely, stored in a protected environment, and regularly rotated to minimize the risk of key compromise. Additionally, key distribution mechanisms must be robust to ensure that authorized parties can securely exchange keys while keeping them out of the hands of attackers.

Cryptographic protocols also play a crucial role in countermeasures. Secure communication protocols, such as Transport Layer Security (TLS), are designed to provide confidentiality, integrity, and authenticity for data transmitted over the internet. These protocols incorporate cryptographic techniques to protect against eavesdropping, tampering, and man-in-the-middle attacks.

Another vital countermeasure is cryptographic hash functions. Hash functions take an input and produce a fixed-size output, often called a digest. They are widely used to verify data integrity and securely store passwords. However, hash functions need to be carefully chosen to resist collision attacks, where two different inputs produce the same hash value, as well as pre-image and second pre-image attacks.

Public key infrastructure (PKI) is another significant component of cryptographic countermeasures. PKI is a framework that provides secure key management, digital certificates, and trust models. It underpins secure communication, digital signatures, and authentication in many modern systems, including web browsers and email clients.

Intrusion detection and prevention systems (IDPS) are critical countermeasures used to monitor network traffic and system activity for signs of malicious behavior. When unusual or potentially harmful activity is detected, these systems can take actions to mitigate the threat and alert security personnel.

Beyond these foundational countermeasures, cryptographic innovations continue to evolve to meet emerging threats. Post-quantum cryptography is a prime example. As quantum computing advances, it poses a unique challenge to existing cryptographic systems. Post-quantum cryptography explores new mathematical principles and encryption techniques that are resistant to quantum attacks, ensuring the long-term security of our data.

Another innovative approach is homomorphic encryption, which allows computations to be performed on encrypted data without decrypting it. This groundbreaking technology has applications in secure cloud computing, enabling data processing while preserving confidentiality.

Furthermore, blockchain technology has introduced a new paradigm for cryptographic security. Blockchains rely on cryptographic hashing and digital signatures to create immutable ledgers. While initially developed for cryptocurrencies like Bitcoin, blockchain technology is now being adopted for various applications, including supply chain management, voting systems, and decentralized finance.

Biometric authentication is another area where cryptographic countermeasures are making strides. By combining cryptographic techniques with biometric data like fingerprints or facial recognition, systems can provide robust and convenient user authentication.

As the Internet of Things (IoT) continues to grow, cryptographic protocols tailored to IoT devices are essential countermeasures. These protocols must balance security and resource constraints to protect interconnected devices from being compromised and used in large-scale attacks.

In addition to these technical countermeasures, user education and awareness play a crucial role in overall cybersecurity. Phishing attacks, social engineering, and password reuse are persistent threats that can undermine even the most robust cryptographic defenses. Educating users about best practices and the importance of strong, unique passwords can significantly enhance the security posture of an organization.

Moreover, regular security assessments, including penetration testing and vulnerability scanning, are essential cryptographic countermeasures. These assessments help identify weaknesses in systems and applications, allowing organizations to proactively address security issues before they can be exploited by attackers.

In the face of ever-evolving threats, it is essential to view cryptographic countermeasures as an ongoing process rather than a static solution. Security technologies and practices must adapt to new challenges and emerging technologies to maintain the confidentiality, integrity, and availability of sensitive data and communication channels.

In summary, cryptographic countermeasures form the bedrock of modern information security. These countermeasures encompass a broad range of technologies and practices, including key management, secure communication protocols, hash functions, PKI, intrusion detection systems, and innovative cryptographic approaches like post-quantum cryptography and homomorphic encryption. Additionally, user education, security assessments, and the adoption of emerging technologies like blockchain and biometric authentication all contribute to the holistic defense of our digital world. As threats continue to evolve, the vigilance and adaptability of cryptographic countermeasures remain paramount in safeguarding our data and digital interactions.

In the ever-evolving landscape of cybersecurity, developing robust defense strategies for cryptographic systems is paramount to safeguarding sensitive data and digital communication channels from malicious actors. These strategies encompass a multifaceted approach that combines technical measures, user education, proactive monitoring, and adaptability to emerging threats.

One fundamental aspect of defense strategies is the concept of defense in depth. This principle involves layering multiple security measures to provide comprehensive protection. Just as a medieval castle had outer walls, moats, and inner fortifications to deter intruders, modern cryptographic systems should employ various layers of security controls to deter and mitigate attacks.

One critical element of defense strategies is cryptographic key management. Properly managing cryptographic keys is essential for the security of any cryptographic system. This includes secure key generation, storage, distribution, rotation, and revocation. Robust key management practices ensure that encryption keys remain confidential and uncompromised, even in the face of determined attackers.

Encryption is a cornerstone of defense strategies, as it safeguards data both at rest and in transit. Full-disk encryption, for example, ensures that data stored on devices remains protected, even if the physical device falls into the wrong hands. Transport Layer Security (TLS) and similar protocols secure data transmission over the internet, preventing eavesdropping and tampering.

Secure communication protocols are another crucial component of defense strategies. These protocols, such as TLS, provide confidentiality, integrity, and authenticity for data exchanged over the internet. By encrypting data and verifying the identity of communicating parties, these protocols protect against eavesdropping and man-in-the-middle attacks.

Intrusion detection and prevention systems (IDPS) are vital for monitoring network traffic and system activity. These systems use various techniques, including signature-based detection, anomaly detection, and heuristics, to identify suspicious or malicious behavior. When potential threats are detected, IDPS can take actions to mitigate them and alert security personnel.

User education is a fundamental aspect of defense strategies. Even the most advanced security technologies can be undermined by human error. Phishing attacks, social engineering, and password reuse are persistent threats that can compromise security. Educating users about these risks and promoting best practices, such as strong and unique passwords, significantly enhances the overall security posture.

Regular security assessments, including penetration testing and vulnerability scanning, are essential components of defense strategies. These assessments help organizations identify and address security weaknesses before malicious actors can exploit them. By proactively identifying vulnerabilities and weaknesses, organizations can reduce the risk of security breaches.

In the face of emerging threats, defense strategies must adapt and evolve. Post-quantum cryptography is an example of an evolving defense strategy. As quantum computing advances, it poses a unique challenge to existing cryptographic systems. Post-quantum cryptography explores new mathematical principles and encryption techniques that are resistant to quantum attacks, ensuring the long-term security of data.

Blockchain technology represents another innovative defense strategy. Blockchains rely on cryptographic hashing and digital signatures to create immutable ledgers. This technology has applications in supply chain management, voting systems, and decentralized finance, providing transparent and secure transaction records.

Biometric authentication is becoming increasingly important in defense strategies. By combining cryptographic techniques with biometric data, such as fingerprints or facial recognition, systems can provide robust and convenient user authentication. This approach enhances security while simplifying the user experience.

Intrusion response and incident management are critical aspects of defense strategies. Despite best efforts, security incidents can occur. Organizations must have well-defined incident response plans in place to minimize damage, investigate incidents, and recover from security breaches efficiently.

As the Internet of Things (IoT) continues to grow, defense strategies must adapt to protect interconnected devices from compromise. IoT security protocols and standards must balance security and resource constraints to ensure the integrity and confidentiality of data exchanged between devices.

In summary, developing robust defense strategies for cryptographic systems is a dynamic and multifaceted endeavor. These strategies encompass key management, encryption, secure communication protocols, intrusion detection, user education, security assessments, and the adoption of emerging technologies like post-quantum cryptography, blockchain, and biometric authentication. As the threat landscape evolves, so must these defense strategies to maintain the confidentiality, integrity, and availability of sensitive data and digital communication channels. Vigilance, adaptability, and a proactive approach are paramount in the ongoing effort to protect against cyber threats and ensure the security of our digital world.

BOOK 4
CUTTING-EDGE CRYPTOGRAPHY
EMERGING TRENDS AND FUTURE DIRECTIONS

ROB BOTWRIGHT

Chapter 1: The Evolving Landscape of Cryptography

Cryptography, the art and science of securing communication, has a rich and fascinating history that spans thousands of years. Its evolution reflects humanity's constant quest for privacy, security, and the protection of sensitive information. To understand the modern landscape of cryptography, it is essential to journey back in time and explore its historical development.

The origins of cryptography can be traced back to ancient civilizations. The earliest known instances of cryptographic techniques date back to ancient Egypt and Mesopotamia, where hieroglyphs and cuneiform symbols were used to encode messages. These early methods were rudimentary, primarily focusing on obscuring the meaning of messages to maintain confidentiality.

One of the most famous examples of ancient cryptography is the Caesar cipher, attributed to Julius Caesar. In this simple substitution cipher, each letter in the plaintext is shifted a fixed number of positions down or up the alphabet. While it was not highly secure, it demonstrated the idea of using algorithms to encode messages.

The Middle Ages saw the emergence of more sophisticated cryptographic techniques, often used for military and diplomatic purposes. The scytale, a device used by the Spartans, involved wrapping a strip of parchment around a rod of a specific diameter and writing the message lengthwise. When unwrapped from a rod of the same diameter, the message became legible. This method introduced the concept of using a shared secret (the rod's diameter) to decode a message.

During the Renaissance, cryptography experienced significant advancements. The Italian polymath Leon Battista Alberti developed the first polyalphabetic cipher, allowing different letters in the plaintext to be substituted with multiple corresponding letters in the ciphertext. This innovation made the encryption more robust and resistant to frequency analysis.

In the 16th century, the Vigenère cipher, named after the French diplomat Blaise de Vigenère, introduced the concept of using a keyword to determine the shift applied to each letter. This method added complexity to encryption and became a standard for several centuries.

The 19th century witnessed the birth of modern cryptography with the development of the Enigma machine. Invented by German engineer Arthur Scherbius, the Enigma machine was a mechanical device used by the Axis powers during World War II. It utilized a complex system of rotors and electrical connections to encrypt messages, making it extremely challenging to decrypt without knowledge of the machine's settings. The Allies' successful efforts to crack the Enigma code, led by mathematician Alan Turing, marked a significant turning point in the history of cryptography.

The advent of computers in the mid-20th century ushered in a new era of cryptography. With the ability to perform complex mathematical operations quickly, computers enabled the development of encryption algorithms based on mathematical principles. The Data Encryption Standard (DES), introduced in the 1970s, became the first widely adopted symmetric-key encryption algorithm.

Public key cryptography, a revolutionary concept, was independently developed by Whitfield Diffie and Martin Hellman, and later by Ralph Merkle and others, in the 1970s. This breakthrough introduced the concept of using a pair of keys, one for encryption and one for decryption, which allowed secure communication without the need for a shared secret. The RSA encryption algorithm, developed by Ron Rivest, Adi Shamir, and Leonard Adleman, became one of the first practical implementations of public key cryptography.

The 1990s brought about the development of the Advanced Encryption Standard (AES), a symmetric-key encryption algorithm selected by the U.S. National Institute of Standards and Technology (NIST) to replace DES. AES is widely used for securing sensitive data and has become a global encryption standard.

The 21st century has seen cryptography become an integral part of our digital lives. It plays a critical role in securing online communications, financial transactions, and data storage. Cryptographic techniques are used in securing e-commerce transactions, protecting personal information in healthcare and banking, and even in the emerging field of cryptocurrencies like Bitcoin.

The evolution of cryptography has not been limited to encryption algorithms alone. Cryptanalysis, the art of breaking codes and ciphers, has also advanced significantly. Modern cryptanalysts use powerful computers and mathematical techniques to analyze cryptographic systems and identify vulnerabilities.

One of the most exciting developments in cryptography is the field of post-quantum cryptography. As quantum computers become more powerful, they pose a potential threat to existing encryption methods. Post-quantum cryptography explores new mathematical approaches that are resistant to quantum attacks, ensuring the continued security of data in a quantum computing era.

In summary, the historical evolution of cryptography reflects humanity's ongoing struggle to protect information and secure communication. From ancient methods of encoding messages to the development of modern encryption algorithms and the ongoing quest for quantum-resistant cryptography, cryptography has come a long way. Its impact on our digital world is profound, and its evolution continues as we strive to stay ahead of emerging threats in the ever-changing landscape of cybersecurity.

The Impact of Technology on Cryptography has been profound and transformative throughout history. As technology has advanced, so too has the field of cryptography, shaping how we secure information and communicate in the digital age.

In the early days of cryptography, technology was limited to basic tools and manual methods. Ancient civilizations used simple devices, such as rods and parchment, to obscure messages. These early techniques were effective in their time but limited by the available technology.

The advent of mechanical devices, such as the Caesar cipher and the scytale, marked a significant advancement in cryptographic technology. These tools allowed for more complex encryption, relying on mechanical processes to enhance security. The scytale, for instance, leveraged the physical properties of a rod to encode and decode messages.

During the Renaissance, technological innovations in printing and the spread of knowledge contributed to the development of more sophisticated cryptographic techniques. The work of individuals like Leon Battista Alberti and Blaise de Vigenère showcased the importance of technological progress in encryption. Alberti's polyalphabetic cipher, which used multiple alphabets to encode messages, demonstrated the potential of technology to enhance cryptographic security.

The 19th century saw the emergence of the telegraph, a technological marvel that introduced new challenges for secure communication. The need to protect telegraph messages from interception led to the development of cryptographic systems tailored to this medium. The technology-driven demand for secure telegraphy played a crucial role in advancing the field of cryptography.

World War II brought about the Enigma machine, a remarkable technological achievement with profound implications for both encryption and decryption. This electromechanical device employed rotors and complex wiring to encrypt messages, and its breaking by Allied cryptanalysts, including Alan Turing, showcased the pivotal role of technology in codebreaking.

The mid-20th century witnessed the rise of computers, a technological leap that revolutionized cryptography. Computers could perform complex mathematical operations quickly, enabling the development of encryption algorithms based on rigorous mathematical principles. The Data Encryption Standard (DES), introduced in the 1970s, marked the first widespread adoption of a computer-driven symmetric-key encryption algorithm.

Public key cryptography, one of the most significant breakthroughs in modern cryptography, was born out of technological advancements in mathematics and computation. The concept of using pairs of keys for encryption and decryption, made possible by the computational power of computers, opened up new possibilities for secure communication. The RSA algorithm, which relies on the difficulty of factoring large numbers, became a cornerstone of public key cryptography.

The internet and the digital revolution brought cryptography to the forefront of technology-driven security. With the rapid expansion of online communication and e-commerce, secure encryption became essential. Technologies like SSL/TLS (Secure Sockets Layer/Transport Layer Security) protocols provided the secure foundations for web transactions, ensuring data privacy in the digital realm.

The 21st century has seen technology continue to shape cryptography in various ways. Quantum computing, a technological frontier, presents both challenges and opportunities for cryptography. While quantum computers have the potential to break existing encryption methods, they also drive the development of post-quantum cryptography, which leverages advanced mathematical concepts to resist quantum attacks.

The advent of blockchain technology and cryptocurrencies has introduced novel cryptographic applications. Blockchain relies on cryptographic principles to secure transactions and create trust in decentralized systems. Cryptocurrencies like Bitcoin utilize cryptographic techniques for wallet security and transaction verification.

Furthermore, advancements in hardware security modules (HSMs) have strengthened cryptographic key management and protection. These specialized devices provide secure storage and processing of cryptographic keys, safeguarding sensitive data against both cyberattacks and physical tampering.

The integration of biometrics into cryptography is another technological milestone. Biometric cryptosystems utilize unique physical or behavioral characteristics, such as fingerprints or iris scans, for authentication and key management. This fusion of biometrics and cryptography enhances security and user convenience.

Artificial intelligence and machine learning have also found applications in cryptography. These technologies help identify patterns, detect anomalies, and enhance cryptographic protocols, contributing to the ongoing evolution of secure communication.

In summary, technology's profound impact on cryptography is undeniable. From ancient methods relying on rudimentary tools to modern cryptographic systems harnessing the power of computers, technology has been a driving force behind the field's development. As technology continues to advance, cryptography will evolve in response, ensuring the security and privacy of digital communication in an ever-changing technological landscape.

Chapter 2: Post-Quantum Cryptography Solutions

Quantum computing, a revolutionary field of technology, has brought forth a new set of challenges and considerations across various domains.

One of the foremost challenges posed by quantum computing is its potential to break widely used cryptographic algorithms. Traditional cryptographic methods, such as RSA and ECC, rely on the difficulty of certain mathematical problems, like factoring large numbers or solving the discrete logarithm problem, which quantum computers can solve exponentially faster than classical computers using algorithms like Shor's algorithm.

This challenge threatens the security of existing data and communications. With sufficiently powerful quantum computers, adversaries could decrypt sensitive information that was previously considered secure. As a result, there is an urgent need to transition to post-quantum cryptography, which focuses on cryptographic algorithms that remain secure even in the face of quantum attacks.

Another significant challenge is the development and practical implementation of post-quantum cryptographic algorithms. While there are promising candidates, such as lattice-based cryptography and code-based cryptography, their adoption requires rigorous testing, standardization, and integration into existing systems.

Moreover, quantum computers themselves face numerous technical hurdles before they become practical for large-scale cryptanalysis. Building and maintaining stable quantum bits, or qubits, that can perform error-free computations remains a formidable challenge. Researchers are actively working on error-correcting codes and fault-tolerant quantum computing to address these issues.

Quantum-resistant cryptography introduces challenges related to key size and computational resources. Many post-quantum cryptographic algorithms are more computationally intensive than their classical counterparts. This poses challenges for resource-constrained devices, such as IoT devices, where computational overhead and energy consumption are critical considerations.

Quantum-resistant key management also presents challenges. As quantum computers can efficiently search through large solution spaces, generating and securely distributing cryptographic keys becomes more complex. New key exchange protocols and infrastructure must be developed to withstand quantum attacks.

Furthermore, quantum computing impacts the security of blockchain technologies. Cryptocurrencies like Bitcoin rely on cryptographic algorithms for transaction security. The advent of quantum computing could potentially compromise the security of these systems, necessitating upgrades to quantum-resistant cryptography or other countermeasures.

In the realm of national security, quantum computing has implications for secure communication and data protection. Government agencies and military organizations must adapt their cryptographic strategies to ensure the confidentiality and integrity of sensitive information.

Additionally, quantum computing raises ethical and policy challenges. The potential for quantum-enabled surveillance and decryption capabilities poses questions about privacy and civil liberties. Governments and international bodies must establish guidelines and regulations to address these concerns.

Quantum-safe infrastructure and quantum key distribution (QKD) technologies offer potential solutions to quantum computing challenges. QKD leverages the principles of quantum mechanics to enable secure key exchange between parties, with the security guaranteed by the laws of physics. While QKD has limitations related to distance and practical implementation, it provides a promising approach to securing communication in a post-quantum world.

Quantum-resistant cryptography is a multidisciplinary field that requires collaboration among mathematicians, computer scientists, physicists, and engineers. Standardization bodies like NIST (National Institute of Standards and Technology) play a crucial role in evaluating and selecting post-quantum cryptographic algorithms for widespread adoption.

Additionally, organizations and industries must proactively assess their cybersecurity postures and transition to quantum-resistant solutions as needed. This includes upgrading cryptographic protocols, key management practices, and security policies to align with the evolving threat landscape.

In summary, quantum computing introduces significant challenges to the field of cryptography. From the potential compromise of classical encryption methods to the development of quantum-resistant algorithms and the ethical implications of quantum-enabled capabilities, the impact of quantum computing on cybersecurity is profound. Addressing these challenges requires ongoing research, collaboration, and adaptation across various sectors to ensure the security and privacy of digital systems in the quantum era.

As we navigate the transformative era of quantum computing, the search for post-quantum cryptographic approaches is of paramount importance.

One of the promising avenues in this quest is lattice-based cryptography. Lattice problems are mathematically challenging tasks based on the geometry of lattices, and they form the foundation of many post-quantum cryptographic algorithms. These algorithms rely on the presumed hardness of lattice problems to provide security against quantum attacks.

NTRUEncrypt, for instance, is a lattice-based encryption scheme that has gained attention for its efficiency and security. It offers a high level of resistance against quantum attacks and has been submitted for standardization by NIST.

Code-based cryptography is another promising approach. It relies on the difficulty of decoding random linear codes. The McEliece encryption scheme, based on this principle, has a long history and is considered one of the most secure options against quantum adversaries. However, it tends to produce larger ciphertexts, making it less suitable for resource-constrained environments.

Multivariate polynomial cryptography is an area that explores the security of cryptographic systems based on the hardness of solving systems of multivariate polynomial equations. While it offers potentially lightweight cryptographic solutions, it faces challenges in terms of practical implementation and key size.

Hash-based cryptography relies on the security of cryptographic hash functions. The Merkle signature scheme, for example, is a hash-based post-quantum digital signature scheme that offers strong security guarantees. However, hash-based cryptography can be less efficient due to the need for large hash functions.

Supersingular Isogeny Diffie-Hellman (SIDH) is a fascinating area within elliptic curve isogeny cryptography. It leverages the mathematical structure of supersingular elliptic curves to create a secure key exchange protocol. SIDH has the advantage of smaller key sizes compared to some other post-quantum approaches.

Another approach gaining traction is the use of error-correcting codes. These codes are designed to correct errors in transmitted data, and they form the basis of several post-quantum cryptographic schemes. The Rainbow and BIKE cryptosystems, for instance, are code-based alternatives that provide efficient and secure cryptographic solutions.

Signature-based post-quantum cryptography is another area of active research. The XMSS (Extended Merkle Signature Scheme) is an example of a stateful hash-based digital signature scheme that offers security against quantum adversaries. Stateful schemes like XMSS require careful key management but provide robust security.

One of the noteworthy aspects of post-quantum cryptography is its diversity. Unlike traditional public-key cryptography, which relies primarily on mathematical problems like factoring or discrete logarithm, post-quantum cryptography explores a wide range of mathematical constructs and assumptions to ensure security in a quantum world.

It's important to acknowledge the ongoing efforts of organizations like NIST in the standardization of post-quantum cryptography. NIST's Post-Quantum Cryptography Standardization project is a collaborative initiative involving experts from around the world to evaluate and select cryptographic algorithms that will form the foundation of secure communications in the post-quantum era.

Additionally, the development of quantum-resistant cryptographic libraries and tools is crucial for the practical implementation of these post-quantum cryptographic approaches. These libraries aim to facilitate the integration of post-quantum algorithms into various software and hardware systems.

As we transition to a post-quantum world, it's essential for organizations, government agencies, and industries to stay informed about the latest advancements in post-quantum cryptography. They should assess their cybersecurity strategies and consider the adoption of post-quantum cryptographic solutions to safeguard sensitive data and communications against the looming threat of quantum attacks.

In summary, the field of post-quantum cryptography is vibrant and dynamic, with various approaches offering promising solutions to the challenges posed by quantum computing. Whether it's lattice-based cryptography, code-based schemes, multivariate polynomials, hash-based cryptography, or isogeny-based techniques, researchers are diligently working to ensure that cryptographic systems remain secure in the face of quantum adversaries. The future of cryptography lies in these innovative approaches, which will play a pivotal role in securing our digital world in the quantum age.

Chapter 3: Homomorphic Encryption and Privacy-Preserving Computing

In the realm of cryptography, there exists a fascinating concept that is increasingly gaining importance in the modern era: homomorphic encryption.

Homomorphic encryption is a cryptographic technique that allows computations to be performed on encrypted data without decrypting it first.

Imagine being able to send your sensitive financial data to a cloud server, have complex calculations performed on it, and receive the results in an encrypted form that only you can decipher, all without revealing the raw data to anyone else.

This is the power and promise of homomorphic encryption, and in the following paragraphs, we will delve into its inner workings, its significance, and its real-world applications.

At its core, homomorphic encryption hinges on the idea of performing algebraic operations on ciphertexts, thereby producing an encrypted result that, when decrypted, matches the result of the same operations performed on the plaintext.

This ability to manipulate encrypted data while it remains confidential is a groundbreaking departure from traditional cryptographic methods, which require decryption before any meaningful operations can take place.

To better understand the concept, consider a practical example. Suppose you have a sensitive document containing financial information, and you want to find the total amount spent on a particular category without exposing the specific expenses.

Homomorphic encryption would enable you to encrypt this document, send it to a server, and have the server compute the sum of the expenses within the category without ever gaining access to the underlying data.

The server would send you back an encrypted result, which you can then decrypt to obtain the sum, all while preserving the privacy of the original document.

Now, let's explore the underlying mathematics that make homomorphic encryption possible. One of the fundamental building blocks is the concept of a mathematical structure known as a "lattice."

Lattices provide a mathematical framework where encryption and decryption operations can be defined in such a way that certain algebraic properties are preserved. This allows computations to be carried out on encrypted data without revealing sensitive information.

One of the most well-known homomorphic encryption schemes is the Partial Homomorphic Encryption (PHE), which enables a specific type of computation. In PHE, you can perform either addition or multiplication on the encrypted data while maintaining its confidentiality.

However, to perform both addition and multiplication operations on encrypted data, you need a Fully Homomorphic Encryption (FHE) scheme. FHE is more complex and computationally intensive but offers greater flexibility in computation.

For a real-world analogy, think of PHE as a calculator that can only perform addition or multiplication, while FHE is like a general-purpose computer that can execute any mathematical operation.

One of the pioneers in the field of homomorphic encryption is Craig Gentry, who introduced the first fully homomorphic encryption scheme in 2009. Gentry's breakthrough opened the door to a wide range of applications.

Now, let's explore the practical applications of homomorphic encryption. One of the most significant areas is secure data outsourcing. Many organizations are reluctant to move sensitive data to the cloud due to security concerns. Homomorphic encryption allows them to delegate computations on their data to the cloud while keeping the data itself encrypted.

This has implications for industries such as healthcare, where medical records can be processed in the cloud without compromising patient privacy.

Another application is in secure data sharing. Homomorphic encryption can enable secure collaboration on encrypted data. Multiple parties can perform computations on the same encrypted dataset without exposing the raw data to each other.

For example, financial institutions can collectively analyze transaction data for fraud detection without revealing individual customer information.

Furthermore, homomorphic encryption can enhance privacy in machine learning. With the rise of AI and machine learning models, there's a growing need to train models on sensitive data while preserving privacy. Homomorphic encryption can be applied to protect data during the training process.

Additionally, privacy-preserving analytics is a domain where homomorphic encryption shines. It allows organizations to gain insights from sensitive data without violating privacy regulations.

For instance, telecom companies can analyze call records to optimize network performance while ensuring subscriber anonymity.

Homomorphic encryption also plays a crucial role in secure authentication protocols. It can be used to protect biometric data, ensuring that even if the biometric template is stored in encrypted form, it can still be used for authentication without exposing the original biometric data.

In summary, homomorphic encryption is a revolutionary cryptographic technique that enables computations on encrypted data without revealing the underlying information. Its applications are far-reaching, spanning secure data outsourcing, privacy-preserving analytics, machine learning, secure collaboration, and more.

As technology continues to advance and the need for secure and private data processing grows, homomorphic encryption is poised to play a pivotal role in safeguarding sensitive information while unlocking new possibilities for secure and privacy-preserving data analytics and collaboration.

In the digital age, where data has become a valuable commodity, and concerns about privacy are on the rise, the concept of privacy-preserving computing has emerged as a vital area of study and innovation.

Privacy-preserving computing, as the name suggests, focuses on developing techniques and technologies that allow individuals and organizations to use and share data while preserving the privacy of sensitive information. Next, we will explore various applications of privacy-preserving computing and how it is shaping the way we interact with data in the modern world.

One of the primary applications of privacy-preserving computing is in the healthcare sector. Medical data is among the most sensitive and personal information, and maintaining patient privacy is of utmost importance. Privacy-preserving techniques enable healthcare providers to securely share patient data for research, diagnosis, and treatment without exposing individual identities or medical histories.

For example, secure multiparty computation (SMC) techniques allow multiple healthcare institutions to jointly analyze patient data while ensuring that each institution's data remains private and confidential. This collaborative approach has the potential to advance medical research and improve patient care without compromising privacy.

Another critical application of privacy-preserving computing is in financial services. Financial institutions handle vast amounts of sensitive data, including transaction records, customer profiles, and credit scores. Privacy-preserving techniques, such as homomorphic encryption, enable these institutions to perform complex calculations on encrypted data while keeping the underlying financial information confidential.

For instance, banks can use homomorphic encryption to assess a customer's creditworthiness without exposing the customer's financial details. This enhances security and privacy in financial transactions and risk assessment.

The field of data analytics has also benefited significantly from privacy-preserving computing. Many organizations rely on data analytics to gain insights into customer behavior, market trends, and operational efficiency. However, they often face challenges related to data privacy and compliance with regulations like GDPR.

Privacy-preserving techniques, such as differential privacy, allow organizations to extract valuable insights from data while obscuring individual-level details. By adding noise to query results or aggregating data at a higher level, organizations can protect individual privacy while still harnessing the power of data analytics.

For instance, a retail company can use differential privacy to analyze shopping patterns and customer preferences without knowing the exact purchasing history of individual customers.

Privacy-preserving computing is also making inroads in the realm of secure authentication and identity verification. Traditional authentication methods often require individuals to reveal sensitive information, such as biometric data or personal identification numbers (PINs). Privacy-preserving techniques, such as zero-knowledge proofs, enable individuals to prove their identity without disclosing the underlying data.

For example, a person can prove that they are of legal drinking age without revealing their exact birthdate. This has applications in age verification for online services, access control, and more.

Privacy-preserving computing is not limited to specific industries; it has broad applications across various domains. For instance, in the field of telecommunications, privacy-preserving techniques can be used to protect user location data while allowing for location-based services.

Similarly, in the education sector, privacy-preserving technologies can help protect student data while enabling personalized learning experiences and educational research. By using techniques like secure multiparty computation, educators and researchers can collaborate on analyzing student performance data without exposing individual student records.

Furthermore, privacy-preserving computing has significant implications for the Internet of Things (IoT). As IoT devices continue to proliferate, the need to protect the privacy of data generated by these devices becomes increasingly critical. Techniques like edge computing and federated learning enable IoT devices to process data locally or collaboratively without sending sensitive information to centralized servers.

For example, smart home devices can use federated learning to collectively improve their performance while preserving the privacy of user interactions and preferences.

Privacy-preserving computing is also relevant in the context of secure messaging and communication. End-to-end encryption has become the norm for many messaging apps, ensuring that only the sender and receiver can decrypt the messages. However, metadata, such as who communicates with whom and when, can still reveal sensitive information.

Privacy-preserving techniques, like secure multiparty computation and onion routing, offer solutions to protect metadata. This enhances the privacy of communication, making it challenging for third parties to track or analyze communication patterns.

In summary, privacy-preserving computing is revolutionizing the way data is used, shared, and analyzed across various industries and domains. Its applications extend from healthcare and finance to data analytics, secure authentication, telecommunications, education, IoT, and secure messaging.

As concerns about data privacy and regulations continue to evolve, privacy-preserving computing provides a robust framework for organizations and individuals to benefit from data-driven insights and services while upholding privacy and security principles. It is a field of innovation that promises to shape the future of data-driven interactions in a privacy-conscious world.

Chapter 4: Blockchain and Cryptocurrencies

In the world of blockchain technology, cryptography plays a foundational and pivotal role, serving as the bedrock upon which the security and integrity of blockchain systems are built. Blockchain, a distributed ledger technology, is renowned for its decentralized nature, where multiple nodes or computers collaborate to validate and record transactions across a network. However, the open and decentralized nature of blockchains poses significant security challenges, which cryptography helps address.

At the core of blockchain cryptography is the concept of public-key cryptography. Public-key cryptography uses a pair of keys: a public key, which is openly shared, and a private key, which is kept secret. These keys are mathematically related in such a way that data encrypted with one key can only be decrypted with the other key. This forms the foundation for secure transactions and data storage in blockchains.

One of the earliest and most well-known blockchain applications is Bitcoin. In the Bitcoin blockchain, users generate pairs of public and private keys to secure their cryptocurrency holdings. When a user initiates a transaction, they sign it with their private key, providing proof of ownership. Recipients can then verify the signature using the sender's public key to ensure the transaction's authenticity.

The security of these transactions relies on the mathematical properties of cryptographic algorithms, making it extremely difficult for malicious actors to forge transactions or steal funds. Bitcoin's success in securing financial transactions has inspired the adoption of blockchain technology in various sectors.

Beyond Bitcoin, other blockchain platforms and cryptocurrencies have emerged, each with its cryptographic

253

protocols and use cases. Ethereum, for example, introduced the concept of smart contracts, self-executing contracts with the terms of the agreement directly written into code. Smart contracts are powered by Ethereum's cryptocurrency, Ether (ETH), and rely on cryptographic algorithms for their execution and security.

Cryptography in Ethereum enables the creation of decentralized applications (DApps) that can automate various processes, from financial transactions to supply chain management and beyond. These DApps leverage blockchain's immutability and cryptographic security to ensure transparency and trust among participants.

In addition to securing financial transactions and enabling smart contracts, cryptography in blockchain technology also ensures data privacy and confidentiality. Privacy-focused cryptocurrencies like Monero and Zcash employ advanced cryptographic techniques like zero-knowledge proofs and ring signatures to obfuscate transaction details, offering enhanced privacy compared to Bitcoin.

Zero-knowledge proofs allow a party to prove the validity of a statement without revealing any specific details about the statement itself. This property is leveraged in privacy coins to hide transaction amounts, sender and receiver addresses, and transaction history.

Furthermore, blockchain cryptography plays a critical role in ensuring the integrity of data stored on the blockchain. Each block in a blockchain contains a cryptographic hash of the previous block, creating a chain of blocks where altering any single block would require changing all subsequent blocks—a computationally infeasible task. This property guarantees the immutability and tamper resistance of blockchain data.

Blockchain networks often rely on a consensus mechanism to validate and add new blocks to the chain. Cryptographic algorithms, like Proof of Work (PoW) and Proof of Stake (PoS), are used to secure the consensus process and prevent malicious actors from gaining control of the network.

In PoW-based blockchains, miners compete to solve complex cryptographic puzzles, with the first to solve it adding a new block to the chain. PoW's computational intensity deters malicious actors as it requires significant computational resources and energy expenditure.

On the other hand, PoS blockchains use a different approach, where validators are chosen to create new blocks based on the amount of cryptocurrency they "stake" as collateral. The cryptographic algorithms involved ensure that validators have a vested interest in maintaining the network's integrity.

While blockchain cryptography provides robust security, it's not without its challenges and evolving threats. Quantum computing, for instance, poses a potential threat to existing cryptographic algorithms. Quantum computers have the potential to break widely used encryption methods, such as RSA and ECC, by efficiently factoring large numbers.

To mitigate this threat, the field of post-quantum cryptography is actively researching and developing encryption methods that can withstand attacks from quantum computers. These new cryptographic algorithms aim to secure the future of blockchain and digital communication in the quantum era.

Additionally, blockchain networks must continually address security vulnerabilities, software bugs, and potential consensus protocol attacks to ensure the ongoing integrity of the system. The openness of blockchain networks means that they are subject to scrutiny from both well-intentioned developers and malicious actors.

In summary, cryptography is the linchpin of security and trust in the world of blockchain technology. It underpins the security of financial transactions, the execution of smart contracts, data privacy, and the immutability of blockchain data. As blockchain technology continues to evolve and find applications in various industries, so too will the cryptographic techniques that safeguard its integrity and security. Blockchain and cryptography are intertwined, forging a path toward more secure, transparent, and decentralized systems in the digital age.

In the realm of cryptocurrencies, security and cryptographic principles are not just important; they are the very foundation upon which the entire ecosystem is built. Cryptocurrencies, like Bitcoin and Ethereum, have rapidly gained popularity, driven by their promise of decentralized, peer-to-peer transactions, and the security of these transactions relies heavily on cryptographic techniques.

At the heart of cryptocurrencies lies the concept of a blockchain, a distributed ledger that records all transactions across a network of computers. The fundamental challenge blockchain technology addresses is ensuring that these transactions are secure, transparent, tamper-resistant, and resistant to fraud and double-spending.

Cryptographic principles, particularly public-key cryptography, play a central role in achieving these goals. Public-key cryptography utilizes pairs of keys—a public key that is openly shared and a private key kept secret. These keys are mathematically linked in such a way that data encrypted with one key can only be decrypted with the other. This forms the basis for secure digital signatures and secure transactions in cryptocurrencies.

Consider Bitcoin as a prime example. In the Bitcoin network, users generate public and private key pairs. When a user initiates a transaction, they sign it with their private key. The recipient can then verify the signature using the sender's public key, confirming the transaction's authenticity. The security of these transactions relies on the computational difficulty of deriving a private key from a public key, making it extremely challenging for malicious actors to forge transactions.

The cryptographic algorithms that underpin these processes are carefully chosen to provide robust security. In the case of Bitcoin, the Elliptic Curve Digital Signature Algorithm (ECDSA) is used for digital signatures. ECDSA offers strong security with relatively short key lengths, making it efficient for blockchain transactions.

While Bitcoin's blockchain is often described as transparent, with all transactions visible to anyone, the identities of the parties involved remain pseudonymous. User addresses in Bitcoin transactions are represented as long strings of characters rather than real-world identities. This pseudonymity is a privacy feature of cryptocurrencies but does not provide complete anonymity.

Privacy-focused cryptocurrencies like Monero and Zcash employ advanced cryptographic techniques to enhance user privacy. Monero, for instance, uses ring signatures and confidential transactions. Ring signatures allow a sender to mix their transaction with others, making it challenging to determine the true sender. Confidential transactions encrypt transaction amounts, further obscuring transaction details.

Another cryptographic technique used in cryptocurrencies is zero-knowledge proofs, which are at the core of Zcash's privacy features. Zero-knowledge proofs allow one party to prove knowledge of a secret without revealing the secret itself. In Zcash, this is used to prove that a transaction is valid without disclosing sender, recipient, or transaction amount.

Beyond securing transactions and providing privacy, cryptographic principles are also instrumental in the consensus mechanisms that govern cryptocurrencies. Bitcoin, for example, employs the Proof of Work (PoW) consensus mechanism. Miners compete to solve complex cryptographic puzzles, with the first to solve it adding a new block to the blockchain. PoW's computational intensity makes it prohibitively difficult for malicious actors to manipulate the network.

Other cryptocurrencies use different consensus mechanisms. Ethereum, the second-largest cryptocurrency by market capitalization, is in the process of transitioning from PoW to Proof of Stake (PoS). PoS relies on validators who are chosen to create new blocks based on the amount of cryptocurrency they "stake" as collateral. PoS systems use cryptographic algorithms to ensure that validators have a vested interest in maintaining the network's integrity.

Despite the robust security provided by cryptographic principles, the world of cryptocurrencies is not without its challenges and threats. Quantum computing, for instance, poses a potential threat to existing cryptographic algorithms. Quantum computers have the potential to break widely used encryption methods, such as RSA and ECC, by efficiently factoring large numbers.

To mitigate this threat, researchers in the field of post-quantum cryptography are actively developing new encryption methods that can withstand attacks from quantum computers. These algorithms aim to secure the future of cryptocurrencies and digital communication in the quantum era.

Furthermore, cryptocurrencies are not immune to software vulnerabilities, hacks, and attacks. Smart contracts, self-executing contracts with terms directly written into code, have become a prominent feature of blockchain platforms like Ethereum. However, vulnerabilities in smart contracts have led to significant losses due to exploits.

Security audits, code reviews, and best practices in software development are essential to minimize these risks. The decentralized and open-source nature of blockchain projects means that vulnerabilities can be discovered and fixed by a global community of developers and security experts.

In summary, security and cryptographic principles are the cornerstones of cryptocurrencies, ensuring the integrity, transparency, and privacy of blockchain transactions. Public-key cryptography, digital signatures, and cryptographic algorithms are used to secure transactions, while advanced techniques like zero-knowledge proofs and ring signatures enhance user privacy. Cryptocurrencies also rely on robust consensus mechanisms like PoW and PoS to maintain network integrity.

Despite the challenges posed by quantum computing and potential vulnerabilities, the cryptocurrency space continues to evolve, with researchers and developers actively working to address these issues. As cryptocurrencies gain wider adoption and find applications beyond digital currencies, the importance of cryptographic principles in ensuring trust and security in the digital realm becomes increasingly evident. Cryptocurrencies represent a paradigm shift in finance and technology, and cryptography remains at the heart of this transformative journey.

Chapter 5: Zero-Knowledge Proofs and Secure Authentication

Zero-knowledge proofs, an intriguing concept in the field of cryptography, offer a powerful way to demonstrate knowledge or possession of information without revealing the actual information itself. These cryptographic constructs have found a wide range of applications in fields as diverse as blockchain, cybersecurity, and privacy preservation.

At their core, zero-knowledge proofs allow one party, the prover, to convince another party, the verifier, that a statement is true without revealing any specifics about the statement. Imagine a scenario where Alice wants to prove to Bob that she knows the solution to a complex mathematical problem without disclosing the solution itself. Zero-knowledge proofs enable Alice to achieve this seemingly magical feat.

The foundations of zero-knowledge proofs rest on three essential properties: completeness, soundness, and zero-knowledge.

Completeness ensures that if the statement is true, an honest prover can convince an honest verifier.

Soundness guarantees that dishonest provers cannot convince honest verifiers of false statements.

Zero-knowledge is the most fascinating property. It asserts that even after interacting with the prover, the verifier learns nothing about the secret, except that the statement is true.

To better understand zero-knowledge proofs, consider the classic example of the "coloring problem." Imagine Alice wants to prove to Bob that she has colored a map with four colors in such a way that no two adjacent regions have the same color. This is a graph theory problem, and Alice wants to convince Bob of her claim without revealing the actual color assignment.

In this scenario, Alice can use a zero-knowledge proof called a "graph isomorphism" proof. She can interact with Bob, providing him with a series of steps that involve rearranging the colors of the regions and swapping them, all while preserving the no-same-color-adjacent rule. If Bob is curious about the validity of Alice's claim, he can request additional rounds of this process. After several iterations, if Alice consistently manages to perform these color swaps without violating the rule, Bob becomes increasingly convinced that her original statement is true.

The beauty of zero-knowledge proofs is that, even after numerous iterations, Bob still has no information about the specific color assignment on Alice's map. He only knows that Alice can perform these transformations consistently, satisfying the zero-knowledge property.

Zero-knowledge proofs find application in various real-world scenarios, most notably in the realm of blockchain and cryptocurrency. One prominent example is the privacy-focused cryptocurrency Zcash. Zcash employs a zero-knowledge proof called zk-SNARKs (Zero-Knowledge Succinct Non-Interactive Arguments of Knowledge) to enable fully shielded transactions.

In Zcash, a sender can prove to the network that they know the necessary information to spend a certain amount of cryptocurrency without revealing the sender, recipient, or transaction amount. This ensures transaction privacy and confidentiality while still maintaining the integrity and security of the blockchain.

Zero-knowledge proofs also play a crucial role in enhancing cybersecurity. Password authentication is a common use case where zero-knowledge proofs can improve security. Instead of sending plaintext passwords to a server, a user can use a zero-knowledge proof to demonstrate knowledge of the password without exposing the password itself. This protects against password leaks or server breaches where passwords might be exposed.

In addition to privacy and security, zero-knowledge proofs have applications in digital identity verification. Consider a scenario where a user needs to prove their age to access certain online content without revealing their exact birthdate. Zero-knowledge proofs can be employed to establish that the user is above a certain age threshold without disclosing the birthdate.

Another fascinating application is in supply chain management and certification. For instance, a producer might want to prove that their product meets certain quality standards without revealing any proprietary information about the production process. Zero-knowledge proofs allow the producer to make this proof while preserving trade secrets.

The potential applications of zero-knowledge proofs are vast and continue to expand as researchers and developers explore new use cases. From secure multi-party computation to anonymous voting systems, zero-knowledge proofs offer a versatile toolset for building trust and security in digital interactions.

However, it's worth noting that while zero-knowledge proofs provide powerful privacy and security benefits, they also come with computational overhead. Verifying zero-knowledge proofs can be computationally intensive, which may impact the performance of systems that use them.

In summary, zero-knowledge proofs are a fascinating cryptographic concept that enables one party to prove knowledge or possession of information without revealing the information itself. They are built on the principles of completeness, soundness, and zero-knowledge, making them a powerful tool for privacy preservation, security enhancement, and trust-building in various domains, including blockchain, cybersecurity, and digital identity verification. As technology evolves, the applications of zero-knowledge proofs will likely continue to expand, offering innovative solutions to complex problems in the digital age.

Authentication, a fundamental pillar of cybersecurity, plays a crucial role in ensuring the identity of users, systems, and entities in digital interactions. In an increasingly interconnected world, where sensitive information is transmitted and stored online, the need for secure authentication protocols has never been more significant. Cryptographic techniques, with their robust security foundations, offer a reliable means to achieve secure authentication.

To understand the importance of secure authentication, one must first recognize the risks associated with unauthorized access. Unauthorized access to sensitive data can lead to data breaches, financial losses, and even compromise the privacy and safety of individuals. Consequently, organizations and individuals alike seek authentication mechanisms that are not only reliable but also resistant to attacks.

One of the simplest and most widely used authentication methods is the use of passwords. Users provide a combination of characters as their "secret" and present it during the login process. However, passwords have significant vulnerabilities, such as susceptibility to brute-force attacks and the potential for user error. In response to these limitations, cryptographic techniques come into play.

Cryptographic authentication protocols enhance security by introducing elements of encryption and digital signatures. One of the most common cryptographic authentication protocols is the Transport Layer Security (TLS) protocol, which is widely used to secure data transmission over the internet. TLS ensures the confidentiality, integrity, and authenticity of data by encrypting it and employing digital certificates to verify the identity of servers.

In TLS, a client and server establish a secure connection by exchanging cryptographic keys and certificates. The client verifies the server's identity by checking the server's digital certificate issued by a trusted Certificate Authority (CA). This process ensures that the client is communicating with the intended server and not an imposter. Similarly, the server can authenticate the client if required.

Beyond TLS, another essential cryptographic authentication protocol is the Extensible Authentication Protocol (EAP). EAP is commonly used in wireless networks, virtual private networks (VPNs), and remote access scenarios. It provides a framework for various authentication methods, including password-based, certificate-based, and token-based authentication. EAP ensures secure authentication by leveraging cryptographic techniques to protect credentials and data during the authentication process.

In the context of cryptographic authentication, digital certificates play a pivotal role. A digital certificate is a tamper-proof electronic document that binds a public key to an individual, device, or service. Certificates are issued by trusted CAs, which vouch for the authenticity of the certificate holder. When a user or system presents a digital certificate during authentication, the relying party can verify the certificate's authenticity using the CA's public key. This trust model ensures that only legitimate certificate holders gain access.

Public Key Infrastructure (PKI) is a comprehensive framework for managing digital certificates and cryptographic keys. PKI provides the infrastructure necessary for secure authentication and key exchange. It includes components like Certificate Authorities, Registration Authorities, and repositories for storing certificates and keys. PKI is widely used in secure communication, email encryption, and digital signatures, making it a cornerstone of cryptographic authentication.

Multi-factor authentication (MFA) is another critical aspect of secure authentication. MFA combines two or more authentication factors to enhance security. The three primary authentication factors are something you know (e.g., password), something you have (e.g., a smart card or mobile device), and something you are (e.g., biometric data like fingerprints or facial recognition). Cryptographic techniques are often used to secure the transmission and storage of these factors.

Biometric authentication, a subset of MFA, relies on unique physical or behavioral traits to verify identity. Biometric data, such as fingerprints, iris scans, or facial features, is captured and converted into digital representations for authentication purposes. Cryptographic techniques ensure the confidentiality and integrity of biometric data to prevent tampering or theft.

One prevalent use case of cryptographic authentication in biometrics is mobile device security. Many smartphones and tablets support fingerprint or facial recognition as a means to unlock the device. The biometric data is securely stored and processed within a Trusted Execution Environment (TEE) on the device, protected by cryptographic keys and secure hardware.

Another cryptographic authentication technique is the use of one-time passwords (OTP) generated through cryptographic algorithms. OTPs are temporary, single-use codes that provide an additional layer of security. They are commonly used in online banking, two-factor authentication (2FA), and secure access to applications. OTPs can be generated using cryptographic algorithms that combine a secret key and a timestamp to produce a unique code for each authentication attempt.

The concept of challenge-response protocols is another vital aspect of cryptographic authentication. In a challenge-response protocol, a verifier challenges a claimant to prove their identity by responding correctly to a cryptographic challenge. These challenges can take various forms, such as random strings or mathematical problems. Cryptographic techniques ensure that the responses provided by the claimant are valid and correspond to their identity.

The Kerberos authentication protocol is a well-known example of a challenge-response protocol used in network authentication. It relies on cryptographic tickets to verify the identity of users and services. When a user requests access to a service, Kerberos issues a ticket granting ticket (TGT) that the user can present to obtain a service ticket. These tickets are encrypted to protect against eavesdropping and unauthorized access.

In summary, secure authentication protocols using cryptographic techniques are essential for safeguarding digital interactions in an increasingly interconnected world. Cryptographic authentication enhances the security of traditional password-based methods by introducing encryption, digital certificates, and multi-factor authentication. These protocols are foundational in ensuring the confidentiality, integrity, and authenticity of data and users in various applications, from online banking to mobile device security. As technology continues to evolve, cryptographic authentication will remain a critical component of cybersecurity strategies worldwide.

Chapter 6: Multi-Party Computation and Secure Collaboration

In the world of cryptography and secure computing, the concept of multi-party computation (MPC) stands as a testament to the ongoing pursuit of privacy and security. MPC is a revolutionary approach that allows multiple parties to jointly compute a function over their private inputs while keeping those inputs secret from each other. This intriguing field of cryptography holds the promise of addressing complex real-world problems without compromising data confidentiality, making it a topic of great significance.

At its core, multi-party computation is rooted in the desire to perform computations collaboratively while ensuring that no single party gains access to the private information of others. The foundation of MPC is based on cryptographic techniques, mathematical protocols, and clever algorithms that enable secure computation in distributed settings. It's as if you're engaging in a group discussion where each participant can reveal their thoughts without exposing their innermost secrets.

One fundamental concept in MPC is the idea of "secure function evaluation." In this context, a secure function refers to any computation that multiple parties want to perform jointly while preserving the privacy of their respective inputs. Imagine a scenario where two medical researchers want to combine their datasets to discover new insights about a disease without revealing sensitive patient information. Secure function evaluation allows them to achieve this goal.

To grasp the essence of MPC, it's essential to understand the "Yao's Millionaires' Problem," a classic example used to illustrate the concept. In this problem, two millionaires, Alice and Bob, want to know who is wealthier without disclosing their actual net worth to each other. MPC protocols enable them to compare their wealth while keeping the exact figures hidden. This example showcases the power of secure computation in maintaining privacy.

The cryptographic techniques underpinning MPC can be divided into two categories: secret sharing and secure protocols. Secret sharing involves dividing a piece of confidential information into multiple shares, distributing these shares among the parties, and ensuring that the original information can only be reconstructed when a sufficient number of shares are combined. This approach forms the basis for many MPC protocols.

Secure protocols, on the other hand, rely on complex cryptographic algorithms to enable parties to jointly compute a function without revealing their private inputs. These protocols often employ advanced mathematical concepts, such as homomorphic encryption, oblivious transfer, and zero-knowledge proofs. They ensure that computations occur in a way that conceals sensitive data even from the parties involved in the computation.

One of the earliest groundbreaking works in MPC was the celebrated "Yao's Millionaires' Problem" solution by Andrew Yao in the 1980s. Yao's protocol demonstrated the feasibility of secure function evaluation and laid the foundation for the development of more practical and efficient MPC protocols over the years. Yao's insight into "secure two-party computation" marked a significant milestone in the field.

Multi-party computation finds applications across a wide range of domains, offering solutions to complex problems while preserving privacy. Consider the healthcare sector, where medical institutions can collaborate to analyze patient data without compromising confidentiality. In financial services, banks can jointly compute risk assessments for loan applications without exposing customer financial data. Even in online voting systems, MPC can enable secure electronic voting while protecting individual choices.

The privacy-preserving nature of MPC has also found relevance in privacy-centric cryptocurrencies. Projects like Zcash and Monero leverage zero-knowledge proofs and secure computation techniques to provide transaction privacy, allowing users to transact with confidence that their financial information remains confidential.

The power of multi-party computation extends to data analytics and machine learning. Organizations can collaborate on data analytics projects while keeping sensitive data siloed within their respective domains. Secure computation techniques facilitate collaborative machine learning models, allowing multiple entities to train models on combined datasets without revealing the underlying data.

Challenges in implementing MPC protocols arise due to the inherent complexities of secure computation and the need for high-level cryptographic expertise. These protocols can be computationally intensive, requiring significant processing power and careful optimization for practical use cases. Furthermore, ensuring security against advanced adversaries is an ongoing challenge in the field.

The development of user-friendly tools and libraries for MPC is an active area of research, aiming to make this powerful technology more accessible to a broader audience. While the theoretical foundations are robust, bridging the gap between theory and practical implementation remains a focus for researchers and developers.

In summary, multi-party computation represents a transformative paradigm in the world of cryptography, offering a means to collaborate, compute, and analyze data securely across distributed environments. Its applications span various domains, from healthcare and finance to privacy-centric cryptocurrencies and machine learning. As technology advances and the need for privacy intensifies, MPC continues to be at the forefront of cryptographic innovation, empowering individuals and organizations to unlock the full potential of secure computation while preserving their data privacy. In the ever-evolving landscape of digital communication and collaboration, ensuring security and privacy are paramount. Cryptographic techniques serve as a robust shield against the prying eyes of cyber threats, enabling individuals and organizations to collaborate with confidence in an increasingly interconnected world. Imagine a scenario where two business partners need to exchange sensitive documents over the internet. In the absence of strong encryption, their data would be vulnerable to eavesdropping by malicious actors. Cryptographic techniques come to the rescue by encrypting the data, rendering it indecipherable to anyone without the decryption key. Encryption, a cornerstone of cryptography, plays a pivotal role in securing digital collaboration. It transforms plaintext information into ciphertext, making it unreadable without the corresponding decryption key. This process ensures that even if data transmission is intercepted, the intercepted data remains unintelligible to unauthorized parties. The concept of encryption has a rich history dating back centuries. Early encryption methods were often rudimentary, but as technology advanced, so did the sophistication of cryptographic techniques. In the modern era, cryptographic algorithms like Advanced Encryption Standard (AES) have become the gold standard for securing data.

Secure collaboration doesn't stop at encryption; it also encompasses digital signatures. Digital signatures enable individuals and entities to verify the authenticity and integrity of digital documents or messages. When you receive a digitally signed document, you can trust that it hasn't been tampered with and that it indeed originates from the claimed sender.

Public Key Infrastructure (PKI) plays a pivotal role in implementing digital signatures. PKI employs a hierarchical structure of digital certificates, with a root certificate authority (CA) at the top, to validate the legitimacy of digital signatures. This intricate system ensures trust and security in digital communication. When it comes to secure collaboration, end-to-end encryption is a term that frequently surfaces. It's a robust cryptographic technique where data is encrypted on the sender's end, and only the recipient possesses the decryption key. This means that even service providers facilitating the communication cannot access the content.

Popular messaging apps like Signal and WhatsApp have embraced end-to-end encryption to safeguard user communications. In these platforms, your messages are transformed into ciphertext on your device and only decrypted on the recipient's device. This ensures that intermediaries, including the service provider, can't access your messages.

Cryptographic techniques also find applications in securing collaborative cloud environments. Cloud storage and file-sharing services enable seamless collaboration among users, but they also introduce security risks. Encrypting data before uploading it to the cloud ensures that even if the cloud provider's security is compromised, the data remains confidential.

Multi-party computation (MPC), as mentioned earlier, is another cryptographic technique that enhances secure collaboration. In situations where multiple parties need to jointly perform computations on sensitive data without revealing their inputs, MPC protocols enable this without compromising privacy.

Consider a scenario where medical researchers from different institutions aim to collaborate on a disease study. Each institution has patient data that cannot be shared due to privacy regulations. Through MPC, they can jointly analyze the combined dataset without disclosing individual patient information, thereby facilitating groundbreaking research while preserving privacy.

Secure collaboration extends to the world of online meetings and video conferences. The rise of remote work has amplified the need for secure communication tools. End-to-end encryption, combined with secure key exchange protocols, ensures that virtual meetings remain confidential and free from unauthorized intrusion.

Despite the growing importance of cryptographic techniques in enhancing secure collaboration, challenges persist. One such challenge is the balance between security and usability. While robust encryption can safeguard data, it must also be user-friendly to encourage widespread adoption.

Key management is another critical aspect. Cryptographic systems rely on keys for encryption and decryption, and managing these keys securely is vital. Solutions such as hardware security modules (HSMs) and key management services have emerged to address this challenge.

Furthermore, cryptographic techniques must continually evolve to stay ahead of cyber threats. Cryptanalysis, the science of breaking cryptographic systems, is an ongoing field of research. As attackers develop more sophisticated methods, cryptographic protocols must adapt to counter new threats.

The importance of cryptographic techniques in secure collaboration is exemplified by the ever-increasing volume of digital data and the need to protect it. Whether it's individuals sharing personal information or organizations collaborating on sensitive projects, cryptography serves as a reliable guardian of privacy and security.

In summary, the digital age has brought about a fundamental shift in the way we collaborate and communicate. Cryptographic techniques are the linchpin of secure collaboration in this digital landscape, safeguarding data, ensuring authenticity, and preserving privacy. As technology continues to advance and our reliance on digital collaboration grows, cryptography will remain an indispensable tool in the arsenal of secure communication.

Chapter 7: Quantum-Safe Cryptography

In the ever-evolving landscape of cybersecurity, one of the most significant looming threats is the advent of quantum computing, a technological leap that could potentially undermine the security of existing cryptographic systems. While quantum computing holds immense promise for solving complex problems at speeds unimaginable by classical computers, it also poses a grave danger to the foundations of modern encryption. In this chapter, we'll delve into the quantum threat, explore its implications for cryptography, and discuss the concept of quantum-safe cryptography as a solution to safeguard our digital world.

Quantum computing leverages the principles of quantum mechanics to perform calculations far more efficiently than classical computers. Classical computers process data in binary bits, which can be either 0 or 1. In contrast, quantum computers use quantum bits or qubits, which can exist in multiple states simultaneously, allowing them to explore vast solution spaces in a fraction of the time. This quantum advantage threatens the security of cryptographic systems that rely on the difficulty of certain mathematical problems for their strength.

One of the most well-known cryptographic vulnerabilities posed by quantum computing is its ability to efficiently solve the integer factorization problem. This problem forms the foundation of widely used encryption algorithms like RSA (Rivest–Shamir–Adleman). Quantum computers, particularly those employing Shor's algorithm, can factor large numbers exponentially faster than classical computers. As a result, RSA and other public-key encryption schemes could become obsolete once large-scale quantum computers become a reality.

The security of digital communication relies on the encryption of sensitive information, ensuring that it remains confidential and inaccessible to unauthorized parties. Public-key cryptography, which underpins most secure digital transactions, hinges on the difficulty of problems like integer factorization and the discrete logarithm problem. The advent of quantum computers threatens to unravel these cryptographic safeguards.

Quantum-safe cryptography, also known as post-quantum cryptography or quantum-resistant cryptography, is a field of study dedicated to developing cryptographic algorithms and protocols that can withstand the computational power of quantum computers. The goal is to create encryption methods that remain secure even in the face of quantum attacks.

One promising approach to quantum-safe cryptography is lattice-based cryptography. Lattice problems are considered challenging for classical and quantum computers alike. By designing encryption algorithms based on the hardness of lattice problems, researchers aim to create cryptographic systems that can resist quantum attacks. The security of lattice-based cryptography relies on the difficulty of finding the shortest vector in a lattice, a problem believed to be quantum-resistant.

Another avenue of research in quantum-safe cryptography explores code-based cryptography. This approach relies on the complexity of error-correcting codes, which are mathematical constructs used in data transmission and storage. Certain code-based cryptographic schemes, like the McEliece cryptosystem, are believed to be resilient against quantum attacks. They are based on problems such as the decoding of random linear codes, which are considered challenging for quantum computers.

Additionally, researchers are investigating hash-based cryptography as a quantum-safe alternative. Hash-based signatures and digital certificates are immune to quantum attacks due to their reliance on one-way hash functions, which are believed to be secure even in the quantum era. These cryptographic methods offer a level of post-quantum security.

Code-based, lattice-based, and hash-based cryptography represent just a fraction of the quantum-safe cryptographic solutions being explored. Researchers are also investigating multivariate polynomial cryptography, hash-based signatures, and more. The aim is to diversify the cryptographic toolbox to ensure that, as quantum computing matures, we have robust defenses in place to protect sensitive information.

While quantum-safe cryptography is a promising field, transitioning to these new cryptographic systems poses its own set of challenges. For example, replacing existing cryptographic infrastructure with quantum-safe alternatives is a complex and resource-intensive endeavor. Organizations and governments must carefully plan and execute these transitions to ensure the continued security of their digital assets.

Furthermore, the timeline for the widespread adoption of quantum computers remains uncertain. Quantum-safe cryptography must be developed and implemented before large-scale quantum computers become a practical threat. This requires a delicate balance of proactive preparation without prematurely discarding existing cryptographic systems that are secure against classical attacks.

In this ongoing battle against the quantum threat, collaboration between researchers, governments, and the private sector is crucial. Open standards and transparent development processes are essential to building trust in quantum-safe cryptographic solutions. International efforts to standardize post-quantum cryptographic algorithms are already underway to facilitate this transition.

Quantum-safe cryptography is not just about securing data in the future; it's also about safeguarding the integrity of past communications. Once large-scale quantum computers become available, they could potentially decrypt intercepted communications that were secured with classical encryption, retroactively compromising sensitive information.

As we navigate this critical juncture in the evolution of cryptography, it's essential to emphasize the importance of quantum-safe practices. Organizations and individuals should stay informed about the latest developments in quantum computing and quantum-safe cryptography. They should also take proactive measures to assess their digital infrastructure's vulnerability to quantum threats and develop strategies for transitioning to quantum-safe cryptographic systems.

In summary, the advent of quantum computing presents both incredible opportunities and significant challenges for the world of cryptography. Quantum-safe cryptography emerges as a vital field of research and development, focused on creating cryptographic systems that can withstand the computational power of quantum computers. While the quantum threat looms on the horizon, the collaborative efforts of researchers, organizations, and governments are paving the way for a quantum-safe digital future.

As we embark on the journey to prepare for the quantum threat, one of the critical aspects is the implementation of quantum-resistant cryptographic algorithms. We've discussed the potential vulnerabilities posed by quantum computing to classical cryptographic systems, and now it's time to delve into the practical steps that organizations and individuals can take to secure their digital communications in a post-quantum world.

Implementing quantum-resistant cryptographic algorithms involves integrating these new cryptographic methods into existing systems, applications, and protocols. This transition is a complex process, as it requires careful planning, extensive testing, and a deep understanding of both classical and quantum cryptography.

One of the first steps in implementing quantum-resistant cryptography is to assess the current cryptographic infrastructure. Organizations need to identify the cryptographic algorithms used in their systems, applications, and communication protocols. This includes encryption algorithms, digital signatures, key exchange protocols, and hash functions.

Once the existing cryptographic landscape is understood, the next step is to select suitable quantum-resistant cryptographic algorithms to replace the vulnerable classical ones. As we discussed earlier, various approaches to quantum-resistant cryptography exist, including lattice-based cryptography, code-based cryptography, hash-based cryptography, and more. The choice of algorithms depends on factors like security requirements, performance considerations, and compatibility with existing systems.

After selecting quantum-resistant algorithms, organizations must initiate a gradual transition process. It's essential to ensure that quantum-safe cryptographic algorithms are integrated seamlessly into existing systems to minimize disruptions. This transition should be gradual, allowing for thorough testing and validation of the new cryptographic implementations.

Testing quantum-resistant cryptographic algorithms is a critical phase of the implementation process. Rigorous testing helps identify any vulnerabilities, compatibility issues, or performance bottlenecks that may arise during the transition. This testing should include both functional testing to verify that the cryptographic algorithms operate as expected and security testing to assess their resistance against quantum attacks.

One significant challenge in the implementation of quantum-resistant cryptography is the potential impact on system performance. Quantum-resistant algorithms tend to be more computationally intensive than their classical counterparts. Organizations need to assess the performance implications of transitioning to these algorithms, especially for resource-constrained devices or real-time applications.

In some cases, it may be necessary to optimize the implementation of quantum-resistant algorithms to ensure acceptable performance levels. This optimization may involve custom hardware acceleration, efficient software implementations, or the use of specialized cryptographic libraries designed for quantum-safe cryptography.

Furthermore, organizations should consider the key management aspects of quantum-resistant cryptography. Key management is a crucial component of any cryptographic system, and it becomes even more critical in the context of quantum-resistant algorithms. As quantum computers could potentially break classical encryption and digital signature schemes, organizations must ensure the security of their cryptographic keys.

Quantum-resistant key management involves practices such as generating longer-lived keys, implementing quantum-resistant key exchange protocols, and regularly refreshing cryptographic keys. It's essential to develop key management strategies that are resilient against quantum attacks while also being practical for day-to-day operations.

Additionally, organizations should stay informed about the latest developments in the field of quantum-resistant cryptography. Cryptographic research is ongoing, and new algorithms and protocols are continually being developed and evaluated. Staying up-to-date with these advancements ensures that organizations can adapt their cryptographic strategies as needed.

Collaboration and standardization are essential in the implementation of quantum-resistant cryptography. Many international efforts are underway to standardize post-quantum cryptographic algorithms to ensure interoperability and security. Organizations should actively participate in these efforts and adhere to recognized standards to facilitate the adoption of quantum-safe cryptographic solutions.

Moreover, it's crucial to consider the broader ecosystem of cryptographic implementations. This includes the adoption of quantum-resistant algorithms in communication protocols, such as TLS (Transport Layer Security) for secure web communication, and in digital certificate infrastructures like PKI (Public Key Infrastructure). Ensuring compatibility with these broader systems is essential for comprehensive security.

In summary, the implementation of quantum-resistant cryptographic algorithms is a multifaceted endeavor that requires careful planning, testing, optimization, and key management. As quantum computing continues to advance, organizations and individuals must take proactive steps to secure their digital communications. The transition to quantum-resistant cryptography is not a matter of if but when, and the time to prepare is now. By embracing quantum-resistant cryptographic solutions and staying engaged in the evolving field of cryptography, we can navigate the quantum threat and ensure the continued security of our digital world.

Chapter 8: Biometric Cryptosystems and Authentication

Biometrics and cryptography, when combined, form a powerful and versatile duo in the realm of security and authentication. These two distinct fields, each with its own set of capabilities and limitations, come together to create a robust framework for safeguarding sensitive information, securing access to systems and services, and ensuring the privacy and integrity of data.

Biometrics, as the name suggests, involves the measurement and analysis of biological and behavioral characteristics unique to individuals. These characteristics can include fingerprints, facial features, iris patterns, voice, hand geometry, and even behavioral traits like keystroke dynamics and gait. What makes biometrics particularly compelling is the inherent uniqueness and stability of these features. Unlike passwords or traditional tokens, which can be forgotten or lost, biometric traits remain constant throughout a person's life.

The marriage of biometrics and cryptography begins with the need to protect biometric templates and the biometric data itself. While biometric traits are unique and stable, they are not entirely immune to attacks or theft. If biometric data is compromised, it can have severe consequences for an individual's privacy and security. To address this challenge, cryptographic techniques are employed to secure biometric data and templates.

One fundamental application of cryptography in biometrics is template protection. When you enroll your biometric data with a system, a template is created based on your unique biometric features. This template is a mathematical representation of your biometric trait, and it must be stored securely to prevent unauthorized access. Cryptography ensures that these templates are encrypted and can only be decrypted by authorized entities.

Furthermore, cryptographic hash functions are employed to protect the integrity of biometric templates. Hash functions take the biometric template and generate a fixed-length string of characters, known as a hash value. Even a small change in the biometric template will result in a vastly different hash value. By comparing hash values, systems can detect whether a biometric template has been tampered with or altered.

Another vital aspect of combining biometrics and cryptography is the secure transmission and storage of biometric data. When you use your biometric trait to gain access to a system or service remotely, such as unlocking your smartphone with a fingerprint, encryption plays a pivotal role in safeguarding the communication between your device and the authentication server. This encryption ensures that your biometric data is not intercepted or tampered with during transmission.

In addition to authentication and access control, biometrics and cryptography are instrumental in addressing the issue of identity theft and fraud. Biometric authentication methods, such as fingerprint or facial recognition, offer a high level of confidence in verifying a person's identity. However, it's essential to ensure that biometric templates and data are not susceptible to theft or replication.

Here, cryptographic techniques like digital signatures come into play. Digital signatures can be used to bind biometric data to a specific individual securely. When a person's biometric data is captured and enrolled, it can be signed with a digital signature to create a secure link between the data and the person's identity. If someone attempts to use the biometric data for fraudulent purposes, the digital signature can be used to verify the authenticity of the data.

Moreover, cryptographic protocols are employed to protect the privacy of individuals during the biometric authentication process. In scenarios where biometric data needs to be matched against a database of enrolled templates, privacy-preserving techniques are used. These techniques ensure that sensitive biometric information is not disclosed or shared unnecessarily, preserving the anonymity of individuals while still allowing for secure authentication.

One of the noteworthy advantages of the combination of biometrics and cryptography is the convenience it offers. Biometric authentication methods are often more user-friendly than traditional password-based systems. Users don't need to remember complex passwords or carry physical tokens. Instead, they can use their biometric traits, which are inherently tied to their identity, making the authentication process seamless and efficient.

However, it's essential to strike a balance between convenience and security. While biometrics are convenient, they are not infallible. There is always a small chance of false positives or false negatives in biometric recognition. Therefore, multi-factor authentication, which combines biometrics with another authentication factor like a PIN or password, is often recommended for critical applications.

Another consideration when integrating biometrics and cryptography is the protection of biometric templates at rest. These templates are highly sensitive and should be stored securely to prevent breaches. Advanced cryptographic techniques, such as homomorphic encryption, enable computations to be performed on encrypted biometric data without exposing the data itself, adding an additional layer of protection.

In summary, the fusion of biometrics and cryptography represents a potent synergy in the field of security and authentication. By leveraging the uniqueness and stability of biometric traits and the mathematical rigor of cryptography, we can establish robust systems that not only enhance security but also offer user-friendly and convenient authentication methods. As technology continues to advance, the integration of biometrics and cryptography will play an increasingly vital role in safeguarding our digital identities and data.

In the ever-evolving landscape of cybersecurity and cryptography, biometric authentication has emerged as a crucial component in fortifying the security of cryptosystems and protecting sensitive information. Biometrics, which involves the use of unique physical or behavioral traits to identify individuals, offers a dynamic and robust approach to user authentication and access control. This chapter explores the role of biometric authentication in cryptosystems, shedding light on its advantages, challenges, and applications in enhancing security.

At its core, biometric authentication relies on the inherent and distinctive characteristics that set individuals apart from one another. These traits can encompass a wide array of physical features such as fingerprints, facial patterns, iris scans, and hand geometry, as well as behavioral attributes like voice patterns, typing rhythms, and gait. Unlike traditional authentication methods that rely on something a user knows (like a password) or something a user has (like a smart card), biometrics leverages something a user is—biological and behavioral markers that are both unique and difficult to replicate.

One of the primary advantages of biometric authentication is its ability to provide a high level of security and accuracy. Passwords, even when carefully crafted, can be forgotten, stolen, or easily guessed. Biometric traits, on the other hand, are inherently tied to an individual and remain consistent over time. This makes it exceedingly difficult for unauthorized users to impersonate someone else successfully.

In the context of cryptosystems, biometric authentication bolsters security by ensuring that only authorized users gain access to encrypted data, digital assets, or cryptographic keys. Cryptosystems, which are designed to secure information through encryption and decryption processes, require a reliable means of verifying the identity of users attempting to access encrypted data. Biometrics serves as a powerful tool in this regard, providing a robust and user-friendly method for authentication.

Biometric authentication in cryptosystems typically involves the enrollment of an individual's biometric data, such as fingerprint scans or facial recognition patterns, during a one-time setup process. This data is then converted into a mathematical representation known as a biometric template, which is securely stored and associated with the user's identity. When the user attempts to access encrypted data or perform cryptographic operations, their biometric trait is captured and compared to the stored template to verify their identity.

Additionally, biometric authentication enhances the usability and convenience of cryptosystems. Users no longer need to remember complex passwords or carry physical tokens like smart cards. Instead, they can simply provide their biometric trait, which is something they inherently possess. This streamlines the authentication process and reduces the risk of password-related security incidents, such as password breaches or forgotten passwords.

However, it's important to recognize that biometric authentication is not without its challenges and considerations. One notable concern is the protection of biometric templates and data. Since biometric data is highly sensitive, it must be securely stored and encrypted to prevent unauthorized access. Cryptographic techniques play a crucial role in safeguarding biometric templates, ensuring that they remain confidential and tamper-resistant.

Moreover, there is a need for robust anti-spoofing measures to detect and thwart attempts to impersonate biometric traits using replicas or fake images. Cryptosystems that employ biometric authentication must incorporate liveness detection mechanisms and anti-spoofing algorithms to ensure the authenticity of the presented biometric trait.

Privacy is another key aspect when implementing biometric authentication in cryptosystems. Users may have concerns about the collection and storage of their biometric data, especially in cases where it is managed by third-party service providers. To address these concerns, privacy-preserving techniques can be employed, allowing for secure authentication without the need to store or transmit raw biometric data.

Furthermore, cryptosystems often benefit from multi-factor authentication (MFA), which combines biometric authentication with other factors like a PIN or password. MFA provides an additional layer of security by requiring users to provide multiple forms of verification before gaining access, further reducing the risk of unauthorized access.

In summary, biometric authentication plays a pivotal role in enhancing the security and usability of cryptosystems. By leveraging the unique and consistent traits of individuals, biometrics provides a robust method for verifying user identities and controlling access to encrypted data or cryptographic keys. While challenges such as data protection, anti-spoofing measures, and privacy considerations must be addressed, the integration of biometric authentication in cryptosystems represents a significant step forward in the quest for stronger and more user-friendly security solutions.

Chapter 9: Cryptographic Protocols for IoT and Edge Computing

The rapid proliferation of Internet of Things (IoT) devices and the advent of edge computing have brought about transformative changes to our daily lives and industries, but they have also introduced significant security challenges that can be addressed through cryptographic protocols. In this chapter, we'll delve into the world of IoT and edge devices, exploring the unique security concerns they pose and how cryptographic protocols play a pivotal role in safeguarding these interconnected ecosystems.

IoT devices, ranging from smart thermostats and wearable fitness trackers to industrial sensors and autonomous vehicles, have become ubiquitous in our homes, workplaces, and cities. They collect, process, and transmit data, enabling greater efficiency, convenience, and automation in various domains. However, the sheer volume and diversity of IoT devices create a vast attack surface that malicious actors can exploit.

One of the fundamental security challenges posed by IoT devices is their inherent resource constraints. Many IoT devices are constrained in terms of processing power, memory, and energy resources. These limitations make it challenging to implement robust security measures directly on the devices themselves. Cryptographic protocols come to the rescue by enabling secure communication, data integrity, and authentication while minimizing the computational burden on IoT devices.

One essential cryptographic protocol in the context of IoT security is Secure Sockets Layer (SSL) or its successor, Transport Layer Security (TLS). TLS provides secure end-to-end communication by encrypting data exchanged between IoT devices and backend servers. This encryption ensures that even if data is intercepted during transmission, it remains unintelligible to eavesdroppers. IoT devices use TLS to establish secure connections when sending sensor data, receiving updates, or interacting with cloud services.

Another crucial aspect of IoT security is device authentication. Cryptographic protocols such as X.509 certificates and Public Key Infrastructure (PKI) enable the authentication of IoT devices and ensure that they connect only to authorized servers or services. This prevents unauthorized devices from infiltrating IoT networks or datastreams.

Edge computing, which involves processing data closer to its source, introduces a new layer of complexity and security considerations. Edge devices, such as routers, gateways, and edge servers, play a pivotal role in processing IoT data and executing real-time decisions. However, these devices are also vulnerable to attacks and need to be protected.

Cryptographic protocols can secure communications between IoT devices and edge devices, as well as among edge devices themselves. For example, the Datagram Transport Layer Security (DTLS) protocol, an adaptation of TLS for use with datagram-based communication, is suitable for securing communication within edge networks. It ensures data confidentiality and integrity while accommodating the challenges of unreliable network connections.

Furthermore, edge devices often rely on cryptographic protocols to implement access control mechanisms. Role-based access control (RBAC) and attribute-based access control (ABAC) are commonly used methods to determine who can access edge resources. Cryptographic protocols can enforce access policies by encrypting data or messages with keys tied to specific roles or attributes, ensuring that only authorized entities can access sensitive information.

When deploying cryptographic protocols in IoT and edge environments, key management becomes a critical consideration. IoT devices and edge devices must securely generate, store, and exchange cryptographic keys to establish secure connections and authenticate each other. Key management protocols, such as the Key Management Interoperability Protocol (KMIP) or the Trusted Platform Module (TPM), help organizations manage cryptographic keys effectively and protect them from unauthorized access.

Moreover, IoT ecosystems often involve diverse stakeholders, including device manufacturers, cloud service providers, and end-users. Cryptographic protocols facilitate secure device onboarding and provisioning, ensuring that IoT devices can be securely integrated into the broader ecosystem. These protocols establish trust between devices and entities, making it possible to verify the authenticity and integrity of devices during the onboarding process.

While cryptographic protocols provide robust security mechanisms for IoT and edge devices, it's essential to recognize that security is an ongoing process. Security patches and updates must be regularly applied to address vulnerabilities, and organizations should continuously monitor their IoT and edge environments for signs of compromise. Additionally, security awareness and training should be provided to all stakeholders to ensure that security best practices are followed.

In summary, the widespread adoption of IoT and edge devices has revolutionized various industries, but it has also introduced complex security challenges. Cryptographic protocols play a vital role in securing IoT and edge environments by providing encryption, authentication, access control, and key management mechanisms. These protocols enable organizations to protect sensitive data and ensure the integrity and confidentiality of communications. However, a holistic approach to IoT and edge security, including regular updates and monitoring, is essential to maintain a strong security posture in this rapidly evolving landscape.

As the Internet of Things (IoT) continues to expand its reach into various aspects of our lives, from smart homes and wearable devices to industrial automation and healthcare systems, the challenges and solutions in cryptographic IoT deployments have become increasingly critical to address. Next, we will explore the unique challenges faced when deploying cryptographic solutions in IoT environments and examine the innovative solutions and best practices that can help mitigate these challenges.

One of the primary challenges in cryptographic IoT deployments is the sheer scale and diversity of IoT devices. With billions of IoT devices expected to be in use in the coming years, ensuring that each device can securely communicate and authenticate itself is a monumental task. Cryptographic solutions must be scalable, lightweight, and efficient to accommodate the resource-constrained nature of many IoT devices.

Resource-constrained IoT devices, such as sensors and actuators, often lack the computational power and memory required for complex cryptographic operations. This limitation makes it challenging to implement traditional cryptographic algorithms on these devices. One solution is the use of lightweight cryptographic algorithms, which are specifically designed to perform efficiently on resource-constrained devices while still providing a reasonable level of security.

Another significant challenge is the need for secure key management in IoT deployments. Cryptographic protocols rely on keys for encryption, authentication, and other security functions. In large-scale IoT environments, managing cryptographic keys securely and efficiently becomes a complex task. Key management solutions, such as the use of hardware security modules (HSMs) or key management services, can help organizations generate, store, and distribute keys securely.

IoT devices are often distributed across geographically dispersed locations, making physical security a concern. Physical access to an IoT device can potentially compromise its security. To address this challenge, hardware-based security measures, such as secure boot processes and tamper-resistant hardware, can be employed to protect devices from physical attacks.

Moreover, the IoT ecosystem involves various stakeholders, including device manufacturers, service providers, and end-users. Each entity may have different security requirements and levels of trust. Cryptographic solutions must support a flexible and scalable trust model that allows for secure device onboarding and provisioning while accommodating the diverse needs of stakeholders.

In IoT deployments, secure communication between devices and backend services is essential. Transport Layer Security (TLS) and Datagram Transport Layer Security (DTLS) are commonly used cryptographic protocols for securing data in transit. However, configuring and managing TLS/DTLS certificates for a large number of IoT devices can be complex. Automated certificate management solutions and certificate authorities can streamline this process and ensure that devices always use valid certificates.

The integrity and authenticity of firmware and software updates are critical in IoT deployments. Unauthorized or tampered updates can compromise device security. Code signing and secure boot mechanisms, supported by cryptographic techniques, can verify the authenticity and integrity of firmware and software updates before they are applied.

Furthermore, cryptographic protocols can play a vital role in securing IoT data. Data encryption ensures that sensitive information remains confidential even if it is intercepted during transmission or storage. End-to-end encryption solutions, combined with secure key management, can protect data at rest and in transit.

In IoT environments, edge computing has gained prominence. Edge devices, such as gateways and routers, process data closer to its source, reducing latency and bandwidth usage. However, these edge devices also introduce security challenges. Cryptographic protocols can secure communication between IoT devices and edge devices, as well as among edge devices themselves. Datagram-based cryptographic protocols, like DTLS, are suitable for securing communication in edge networks.

To address the challenge of ensuring device authenticity and integrity, device identity solutions based on digital certificates and Public Key Infrastructure (PKI) can be deployed. These solutions verify the identity of IoT devices and ensure that they connect only to authorized services, reducing the risk of unauthorized access and data breaches.

IoT deployments often involve sensitive data, and regulatory compliance is a significant concern. Cryptographic solutions can help organizations meet regulatory requirements by ensuring data protection and privacy. Compliance with standards such as the General Data Protection Regulation (GDPR) and industry-specific regulations is essential for IoT deployments that handle personal or sensitive data.

In summary, the cryptographic challenges and solutions in IoT deployments are multifaceted, driven by the scale, diversity, and resource constraints of IoT devices. Addressing these challenges requires a holistic approach that combines lightweight cryptographic algorithms, scalable key management solutions, hardware-based security measures, and flexible trust models. By adopting best practices and innovative cryptographic techniques, organizations can enhance the security of their IoT deployments and protect sensitive data in this ever-expanding IoT landscape.

Chapter 10: Ethical and Societal Implications of Cryptography

In the ever-evolving landscape of cryptography, ethical considerations play a crucial role in guiding research and use. Cryptography is not merely a technical field but one that has profound implications for privacy, security, and society as a whole. As we explore the ethical dimensions of cryptographic research and use, it becomes evident that these considerations go beyond the realm of algorithms and protocols.

At the heart of ethical considerations in cryptography is the balance between security and privacy. Cryptographic techniques are employed to safeguard sensitive information and communications, but they can also be used for malicious purposes. Ethical researchers and practitioners must grapple with questions surrounding the responsible use of cryptography and the potential consequences of their work.

One fundamental ethical principle in cryptography is the protection of individual privacy. Cryptography enables individuals to secure their personal data and communications, shielding them from unauthorized access. Researchers and developers have a responsibility to design cryptographic systems that prioritize user privacy and minimize the risk of data breaches.

Transparency is another key ethical consideration. The cryptographic community places great emphasis on openness and the peer review process. Researchers are encouraged to publish their findings, allowing others to scrutinize their work and identify vulnerabilities or weaknesses. This transparency helps ensure the reliability and trustworthiness of cryptographic systems.

However, there is an ethical tension between transparency and responsible disclosure. When researchers discover vulnerabilities in cryptographic systems, they face a dilemma: should they disclose the vulnerability publicly, potentially aiding malicious actors, or should they report it privately to the system's developers for a fix? Striking the right balance between transparency and responsible disclosure is a challenging ethical decision.

Ethical concerns extend to the development of cryptographic standards and protocols. Standards organizations like the National Institute of Standards and Technology (NIST) play a significant role in shaping the cryptographic landscape. Ensuring that these standards are free from backdoors or vulnerabilities that could be exploited by malicious actors is of paramount importance.

Moreover, the ethical use of cryptography in law enforcement and national security contexts raises complex questions. Governments and law enforcement agencies sometimes seek to weaken encryption to facilitate surveillance and criminal investigations. Ethical debates revolve around the trade-off between individual privacy rights and national security interests. Striking the right balance between these competing interests is a recurring ethical challenge.

Cryptography also plays a role in the ethical considerations of cybersecurity. Organizations are ethically obliged to protect sensitive data from cyberattacks, which often involve the use of cryptographic techniques. Negligence in securing data can have far-reaching consequences, impacting individuals' privacy and financial well-being.

Another ethical dimension of cryptography is its role in secure and anonymous communication. Cryptocurrencies like Bitcoin use cryptographic techniques to enable financial transactions without the need for intermediaries. While this offers advantages in terms of privacy and financial autonomy, it also raises ethical concerns related to money laundering, fraud, and illegal activities.

The ethical considerations in cryptography extend to the impact on vulnerable populations. Cryptography can empower individuals in repressive regimes to communicate securely and access information freely. Ethical researchers and developers must consider the implications of their work on human rights and social justice.

Additionally, cryptographic research often involves substantial financial resources. Ethical questions arise concerning how these resources are allocated, who benefits from cryptographic advancements, and whether there is equitable access to cryptographic tools and knowledge.

As artificial intelligence and machine learning become increasingly integrated with cryptography, ethical considerations expand further. Ensuring that cryptographic algorithms and AI systems are developed and deployed in ways that are fair, unbiased, and ethical is an emerging challenge.

In summary, ethical considerations are integral to the field of cryptography. Cryptographers, researchers, and practitioners must grapple with complex ethical dilemmas surrounding privacy, transparency, responsible disclosure, national security, cybersecurity, financial autonomy, and social justice. Striking a balance between security and privacy, transparency and responsible disclosure, and individual rights and national security requires thoughtful deliberation and ongoing dialogue within the cryptographic community. Ultimately, ethical considerations should guide the development and use of cryptographic technologies in a manner that benefits society while minimizing harm. Cryptography, with its ability to secure information and communications, has had a profound impact on society, reshaping the way we interact, work, and conduct business in an increasingly digital world. As we've discussed throughout this book, cryptography plays a pivotal role in safeguarding sensitive data, enabling secure online transactions, and protecting individual privacy. However, this transformative technology is not without its share of privacy concerns and societal implications that warrant careful consideration. One of the primary privacy concerns associated with cryptography is the tension between individual privacy rights and national security interests. Governments and law enforcement agencies often seek access to encrypted data for legitimate reasons, such as preventing terrorism or investigating criminal activities. But the development of strong encryption methods has also made it challenging for authorities to access data, even when warranted by court orders. This has led to debates about whether there should be backdoors or "exceptional access" mechanisms in cryptographic systems to allow lawful interception while maintaining user privacy. The balance between privacy and national security is a complex ethical and legal dilemma that continues to be a subject of intense debate and scrutiny. Cryptography also plays a pivotal role in protecting user privacy in the digital age. End-to-end encryption, for example, ensures that only the intended recipients can access the content of their messages, making it nearly impossible for service providers to intercept or decipher user communications. While this is a significant win for individual privacy, it has raised concerns about the potential misuse of encryption by malicious actors, including criminals and terrorists. As a result, there have been calls for greater transparency and cooperation between technology companies, governments, and law enforcement agencies to strike a balance between privacy and security. Cryptography's impact on society extends beyond individual privacy and national security concerns. In the realm of finance, cryptocurrencies like Bitcoin have emerged as decentralized, secure, and private means of conducting transactions. These digital currencies rely on cryptographic techniques to facilitate secure, pseudonymous transactions, reducing the need for intermediaries like banks. While this innovation has the potential to empower individuals with greater financial autonomy, it has also raised concerns about money laundering, tax evasion, and the lack of regulatory oversight. The ongoing evolution of digital currencies and their intersection with cryptography will likely continue to shape financial landscapes and regulatory frameworks. Cryptography's role in protecting data and privacy extends to various sectors, including healthcare, where electronic health records are increasingly prevalent. The use of encryption ensures the confidentiality and integrity of sensitive patient information, but it also requires robust cybersecurity measures to defend against data breaches and ransomware attacks. While cryptography plays a crucial role in securing healthcare data, it is not immune to the ever-evolving landscape of cyber threats. As encryption techniques become more sophisticated, cybercriminals develop new methods to bypass these security measures, emphasizing the need for continuous innovation and vigilance in cybersecurity practices. The impact of cryptography on society is also intertwined with its role in secure online commerce and e-commerce. Consumers rely on encryption to protect their financial information when making online purchases or accessing banking services. E-commerce platforms, in particular, rely on secure cryptographic protocols to ensure the confidentiality and integrity of transactions. Yet, these platforms are not immune to data breaches and security vulnerabilities, highlighting the ongoing challenges of maintaining robust cybersecurity in the digital marketplace. Privacy concerns also extend to the collection and use of personal data by technology companies, social media platforms, and data brokers. Cryptography can play a role in enhancing user privacy through techniques such as differential privacy, which adds noise to data to protect individual identities while allowing for meaningful analysis. Efforts to strike a balance between data-driven innovation and individual privacy rights have led to regulatory frameworks like the European Union's General Data Protection Regulation (GDPR). Cryptography's impact on privacy and society is not limited to protecting data but extends to the field of secure communication. End-to-end encrypted messaging apps, for instance, offer individuals a level of privacy and security that was previously challenging to achieve. However, the use of such apps by criminals and malicious actors has raised concerns for law enforcement and national security agencies. The debate over whether technology companies should provide exceptional access to encrypted communications remains a contentious issue. The ethical and societal implications of cryptographic technologies go beyond privacy concerns to encompass broader discussions about human rights, freedom of expression, and social justice. In repressive regimes, cryptography can empower individuals to communicate securely, access information, and organize for social or political change. Yet, these technologies can also be used to surveil and suppress dissent, underscoring the dual-edged nature of cryptographic tools in different geopolitical contexts. The impact of cryptography on society is not static but continues to evolve as technological advancements and societal changes shape the landscape. As quantum computing and post-quantum cryptography come to the forefront, discussions about the future of cryptographic security and privacy intensify. Quantum computers have the potential to break current cryptographic systems, prompting researchers to develop quantum-resistant encryption methods. This ongoing dialogue underscores the dynamic nature of cryptography's role in society and the imperative of addressing privacy and security concerns in an ever-changing digital world. In summary, cryptography has had a profound impact on society by enhancing individual privacy, securing digital transactions, and shaping the way we communicate and interact online. While it has raised privacy concerns, ethical dilemmas, and debates about the balance between security and individual rights, cryptography remains an indispensable tool in safeguarding our increasingly digital lives. As we navigate the complex terrain of privacy and societal implications, ongoing collaboration and dialogue among technologists, policymakers, and ethicists are essential to strike the right balance between privacy, security, and the greater good of society.

Conclusion

In the realm of digital security and information protection, the world of cryptography and computer science stands as an indispensable guardian of our digital lives. The journey we embarked upon in this comprehensive book bundle, "Cryptography and Computer Science: Design Manual for Algorithms, Codes, and Ciphers," has taken us through the intricate landscape of cryptographic principles, algorithms, protocols, cryptanalysis, and emerging trends. As we reach the conclusion of this enlightening expedition, let us reflect on the knowledge we've gained and the path ahead.

In "Book 1 - Introduction to Cryptography: A Beginner's Guide," we laid the foundation for our exploration, demystifying the fundamental concepts of cryptography. We learned about encryption, decryption, keys, and the critical role of cryptography in safeguarding sensitive information. It was a beginner's guide that paved the way for deeper insights.

"Book 2 - Cryptographic Algorithms and Protocols: A Comprehensive Guide" delved into the heart of cryptography, unveiling a vast array of cryptographic algorithms and protocols. From symmetric key cryptography to asymmetric cryptography, from block ciphers to stream ciphers, we discovered the diverse tools at the disposal of cryptographers. We explored the protocols that secure our online transactions, communications, and data storage, comprehending their inner workings.

Our journey took an exciting turn in "Book 3 - Advanced Cryptanalysis: Breaking Codes and Ciphers." Here, we wore the hat of cryptanalysts, deciphering encrypted messages and uncovering the vulnerabilities of cryptographic systems. We delved into classical and contemporary cryptanalysis techniques, learning the art of code-breaking and understanding the perpetual battle between cryptographers and cryptanalysts.

"Book 4 - Cutting-Edge Cryptography: Emerging Trends and Future Directions" projected us into the future of cryptography. We explored quantum computing's impending threat and the race to develop post-quantum cryptography. We discussed the exciting developments in homomorphic encryption, multi-party computation, and zero-knowledge proofs. We envisioned a world where cryptography continues to evolve, adapting to the ever-changing digital landscape.

As we draw the curtains on this book bundle, we recognize that the field of cryptography and computer science is not static but dynamic, responding to technological advancements and societal challenges. The knowledge we've acquired equips us with the tools to navigate this evolving landscape and make informed decisions about digital security.

In this age of information and technology, cryptography is the bedrock upon which our digital trust is built. It is a field that bridges the realms of mathematics, computer science, and ethics, serving as both a shield and a sword in the digital world. We've explored its depths, from its theoretical foundations to its practical applications, from its strengths to its vulnerabilities.

As we conclude this journey, let us remember that the quest for cryptographic excellence continues. New challenges will arise, and new solutions will be devised. Cryptographers, computer scientists, and security professionals will continue to innovate, ensuring that our digital interactions remain secure and our privacy protected.

In closing, "Cryptography and Computer Science: Design Manual for Algorithms, Codes, and Ciphers" has been a voyage of discovery, empowerment, and enlightenment. It is our hope that the knowledge imparted within these pages serves as a guiding light in your pursuit of digital security, innovation, and excellence in the realm of cryptography and computer science.

www.ingramcontent.com/pod-product-compliance
Lightning Source LLC
Chambersburg PA
CBHW071234050326
40690CB00011B/2109